THE RUGGED ENTREPRENEUR

The Rugged Entrepreneur
What Every Disruptive Business Leader Should Know

Published by Forefront Books in association with the
literary agency of Wolgemuth & Associates.

Cover Design by Bruce Gore, Gore Studio Inc.
Interior Design by Bill Kersey, KerseyGraphics

ISBN: 978-1-948-67768-4
ISBN: 978-1-948-67769-1 (eBook)

THE
RUGGED
ENTREPRENEUR

WHAT EVERY
DISRUPTIVE
BUSINESS LEADER
SHOULD KNOW

CARLTON SCOTT ANDREW

Forefront
BOOKS

TABLE OF CONTENTS

ACKNOWLEDGMENTS

SAYING "THANK YOU" FOR THE PRICELESS LESSONS THAT SO MANY people helped me learn on my journey to becoming a disruptive Rugged Entrepreneur is almost as challenging as writing a book itself. Considering that challenge, I first wish to thank God for inspiring me to do this and for blessing me with all the wisdom-building experiences (good and bad) that have shaped my life. I am truly grateful for the relationships, examples, opportunities, books, authors, events, successes, failures, and ultimately, for the capabilities that have helped me to empower millions of existing and would-be entrepreneurs. All of those experiences and people are part of this unique accomplishment. Secondly, I must thank my mother and father, and my incredible wife. My parents expected and believed that one should work hard and be good at whatever they decided to do in life. They did not allow my sister or me to quit a hobby or activity until it was finished. My mother also introduced me to the great fun and adventure of reading by encouraging me to spend quiet time in the evenings with a good book. My father and my wife are the two hardest-working people I know. Having the example of my father's work ethic throughout my life and decades of my wife's unwavering commitment to be a phenomenal Rugged Entrepreneur business partner, as well as my number one cheerleader, have meant more to me than this small acknowledgment could ever convey. To these extraordinary people, I say, THANK YOU.

PROLOGUE

"Whether you think you can, or you think you can't, you're right."
—Henry Ford

As I have always said and firmly believe, anyone can become an entrepreneur. Millions of people around the world make the leap every year. However, the majority of them don't know what it takes to succeed before they jump in. And if by chance they do experience early success, they likely don't know how to sustain or consistently build upon that success. Rugged Entrepreneurs (aka, "Ruggeds") have a *totally* different story to tell. Ruggeds make the leap toward success in a way that separates them from the millions who fall short because they have invested the time and effort to develop and hone the specific set of powerful skills you will discover in these pages.

I am a highly successful serial entrepreneur whose adventures in business have touched hundreds of other entrepreneurs in a wide variety of industries. I have worked tirelessly to define and exemplify the meaning of Rugged Entrepreneurialism through my actions as well as through my words. My teams and I have inspired and trained scores of other businessmen and businesswomen to become Ruggeds, too, and now we provide various models and consultative services so entrepreneurs can fashion their own profitable businesses as Ruggeds themselves.

Throughout my career, I have met, studied, and coached numerous developing Ruggeds, millionaire Ruggeds, multimillionaire Ruggeds, and *billionaire* Ruggeds. The differences between them are not that great. In fact, all of the studies I have read and conducted show that between 70 to 80 percent of all Ruggeds—whether they are millionaires or billionaires—are self-made. That being said, the differences between Ruggeds and those who fail to become Ruggeds are enormous. But don't be discouraged. You can bridge the gap if you truly want to. *Anyone* can learn to do the things it takes to become a Rugged Entrepreneur, and this book will show you how.

The following pages *are not* about starting a business, owning a job, or being just another statistic. They *are* about lasting self-discovery. They're about identifying and acquiring the skills to achieve sustained success and to build on top of that success. They're about passionately pursuing a productive business life for yourself and your family using the economic engines accessible to us all. But be warned: do not read this book if you do not want to be challenged. Rugged Entrepreneurialism, by definition, is not for people weak of mind, heart, or commitment. Rugged Entrepreneurialism cannot be summed up in one word or even a short phrase. It is multi-dimensional and one of its demands is that you have the humble grit to finish a task started (such as reading this book all the way to the end).

Bear in mind that Ruggeds come in all shapes and sizes, and the term Rugged is blind to color, race, religion, sex, orientation, educational level, upbringing (including whether you were raised in affluence or poverty), or any other classification. *Blind is blind.* All Ruggeds, however, possess common character traits, habits, and skills. Again, these are traits, habits, and skills *anyone* can develop. Whether you are someone with aspirations to become a Rugged or you have already acquired a few of these qualities on your own and are looking to develop the complete package, this book is for you.

The early chapters cover the foundational elements every Rugged must develop to be sure they have established a solid base upon which to build. Rugged businesses cannot survive, succeed, and thrive without these elements. The latter chapters focus on additional qualities that not only give Ruggeds the ability to design and customize their business as they wish, but also to become market disruptors as they expand and grow.

In a world where business education is often more complicated than it needs to be, the aim of *The Rugged Entrepreneur* is to take a more common-sense approach, presenting concepts as simply and directly as possible. It includes real-life examples, factoids, quotes, analogies, poems, and stories so that the messages and lessons of this book can be more effectively committed to memory and easily accessed later as needed. In ancient times, parables, proverbs, and songs helped make similar emotional connections between messages and memory. People enjoyed using them to pass on wisdom from one generation to the next. What all of these features intend to do here is create rapid-fire associations in your mind, which is referred to today as *emotional word pictures*. These are powerful and instant reminders of what you have learned. I value this type of learning whenever I've encountered it.

Of course, reading is a type of work. It requires a time commitment that most adults are reluctant to make these days. Having the fortitude to complete this book and to act on its contents also require a willingness to think differently, work differently, live differently, and, ultimately, succeed differently. Being a Rugged Entrepreneur will not be easy, and it certainly will not always be fun. It is not for the many. Rather, it is for the determined few. But its rewards, both personal and financial, are many.

If you think you already know everything you need to know about being successful in business, put this book down now and check to see how many people are actually following you. If there are none, or very few, yours is likely to become another number in the statistical heap of failed businesses. Likewise, if you believe you have the very best ideas of all, go to the library or to Amazon and browse the countless number of books that exist in the business section. Then ask yourself: *Do I really have enough gems or even a single original idea that is not already contained therein?* If those two simple mental exercises seem too challenging, you should probably save yourself the pocket change needed to buy this book because becoming a Rugged is likely not for you.

If, however, you truly have a desire to learn, I assure you that a great adventure awaits you. It's one where you can enjoy and be proud of your success, and more importantly, be proud of what you represent. If that is your aim, then know that I sincerely hope this book helps you become the Rugged you are capable of being. I often say, "There is no limit to what a Rugged can do. In that regard, the organizations they build are like skyscrapers." Ruggeds are like the very business "skyscrapers" they build. Their view of the world is clear and expansive. They stand tall and proud. And most of all, they have enormous potential to provide themselves and others greater room and freedom in which to live and work.

—SCOTT ANDREW

BUILDING A SOLID FOUNDATION

CHAPTER ONE

THE FOUR ELEMENTS OF A RUGGED ENTREPRENEUR

"If you have built castles in the air, your work need not be lost; that is where they should be. Now put the foundations under them."
—HENRY DAVID THOREAU

IF WE ARE LUCKY, WE HAVE BEEN TAUGHT TO DREAM SINCE THE TIME we were very young. If we are luckier still, we have also been taught to establish a sturdy foundation for those dreams to stand upon. When building the business of which you've always dreamed, you must first establish a rock-solid foundation. This is especially true if you hope for that business to become a towering success one day. This is how I interpret and apply the quote opening this chapter from Henry David Thoreau to my life. This is also what I've learned from many years of experience as a Rugged Entrepreneur.

Of course, there are exceptions to every rule. The Leaning Tower of Pisa in Italy, for instance, has become one of the most iconic architectural sights in the world even though it is a clear example of a foundation failure. The Millennium Tower in San Francisco is also a noteworthy example of a structure that was built without a proper foundation to support its height and weight despite the huge sum of money spent on it. Since that tower was completed in 2008, it has sunk more than 17 inches and now leans outward by 14 inches. The additional cost of driving hundreds of impact micropiles down to the bedrock to help set that building right is estimated to be as much as $500 million—almost twice its original construction price.

These exceptions are worth noting at the outset of this book for several reasons. First, they remind us of the risk and potential cost of building a business on shaky ground. They also remind us to learn and acquire as many skills as humanly possible to avoid such a fate or to turn mistakes into great success. They emphasize that unanticipated challenges occur in every business as it grows, and that these challenges often reveal the weaknesses in a foundation's structure.

The good news is that some foundations can be modified. If you have already laid a poor foundation, or weaknesses are beginning to show in one that appeared to be sturdy at first, now is the time to recognize this and circle back to fix it. Ruggeds have the fortitude to address and overcome challenges whenever they arise. In the case of the San Francisco's Millennium Tower, the efforts it is taking to correct the foundation's flaws reflect that kind of fortitude. As Dale Carnegie once said, *"Most of the important things in the world have been accomplished by people who have kept on trying when there seemed to be no hope at all."*

But there is another building every Rugged Entrepreneur should be aware of that is definitely worth emulating. A while back during a visit to the United Arab Emirates, my wife, Daphene, and I had the pleasure of touring the remarkable Burj Dubai, which at the time was the tallest building in the world standing 2,722 feet into the air and weighing over

500,000 metric tons. As I stared up at this dazzling, massive structure I couldn't help but think that one of its greatest attributes lies hidden underground. For me, its foundation—built with hundreds of 5-foot-thick cylindrical steel pilings driven 160 feet deep to bedrock and supporting a concrete and steel platform 12 feet thick—is the real feat of engineering mastery in that building's design and execution. Can you just imagine the collective strength these several hundred enormous steel rods represent?

I mention this here because in order to support the massive business you have yet to build as a Rugged Entrepreneur, you will need an uncompromising foundation much like the one these steel rods form. If you think about the word "founder," which is the term most often used to describe an entrepreneur, you will see that it is up to you to *be* the foundation and thus up to you to *build* it. There are several essential qualities that will help you carry the responsibilities of that role and also help you construct a foundation for your business as strong as the Burg Dubai's. I call these qualities *The Four Foundational Elements of a Rugged Entrepreneur*. These elements can be developed by anyone and are helpful to every type of entrepreneur. But remember, *all* four of them are necessary to do the job well. They are:

- A fervent work ethic
- A humble and healthy pride (what I call "Rugged Pride")
- *Fortitudo mentis* (aka, mental toughness)
- Faith

The difference between the steel rod foundation of the Burj Dubai and the foundation built upon the four elements of a Rugged Entrepreneur, however, is that our four elements must be strong enough to support a structure that continues to grow with every passing year. Unlike the architects and builders of skyscrapers, Ruggeds never stop adding stories to their enterprises. Successful Ruggeds are always improving themselves, growing their organization of people, and increasing their portfolio of assets. This is why I say that a fervent work ethic is paramount.

Every time a new story is added to the metaphoric skyscraper that a Rugged is continually building, there are external conditions that must be addressed too. When architects design a building today, they must consider extreme matters of climate change. Their building must be able to withstand hurricanes, fires, floods, tornadoes, and now such unusual occurrences as bomb cyclones. As an entrepreneur continues to build each new level of their business, they must consider the extreme dangers that come from unexpected directions at unexpected times. Succeeding as an entrepreneur is impossible without building an infrastructure to withstand such challenges as competition, liability, dishonesty, shortage of capital, difficult customers, economic downturns, evolving tools of trade, cultural shifts, talent-building, retention issues, supply-chain disruptions, legal obstacles, regulatory changes, technological developments, and many other circumstances that present roadblocks, pitfalls, and threats to success. In the same way that a violent storm of nature can bring a building construction crew to their knees, a violent storm in business can bring an entrepreneur to their knees. This is why I say a measure of a **humble and healthy** pride must be exerted. Here, I am reminded of another favorite quote:

> *"Do you wish to rise? Begin by descending.*
> *Do you plan a tower that will pierce the clouds?*
> *Lay first the foundation of humility."*
> —SAINT AUGUSTINE

In periods of either calm or storm, Rugged Entrepreneurs must remain alert and strong in order to anticipate, avoid, or confront the unique challenges of the business climate in which they find themselves. Because there is strength in numbers, they must not only develop fortitude in themselves, but they must do the same for the others around them. The employees Ruggeds attract and cultivate don't have to bear the full weight of a business the way a Rugged must, but they are nevertheless trained to be an integral part of the organization's foundation. This is why I say **mental toughness** is a vital part of a Rugged's character and the character of his or her team members.

The success of a Rugged Entrepreneur is equal to the size and heft of the structure they build and shoulder. Ruggeds form all sizes of structures and thus cover a broad spectrum of income and net worth. The different degrees of success between a Rugged Millionaire and a Rugged Billionaire have a direct correlation to the amount of responsibility the entrepreneur chooses to accept and, of course, the skill level they possess to handle it. A highly successful Rugged Entrepreneur must develop a stronger, broader, and deeper foundation than leaders in many other types of organizations because the success of a Rugged is not derived from following a traditional career path. They are building *from scratch*, so to speak. Common sense dictates that the stronger, broader, and deeper the foundation, the more that can be built upon and supported by it. To be so bold a Rugged Entrepreneur must plan well and believe in their plan enough to invest their resources of time, money, and passion. This is why I say **faith** is also an essential element of being a Rugged Entrepreneur.

Rugged Millionaires generally build one or two small skyscrapers. For example, they may build either one hotel, one restaurant, one e-commerce business, or one distribution company. But Rugged Billionaires generally go way beyond building a singular business. Look at the self-made Rugged Billionaire Peter Stordalen, who has approximately 200 hotels, as well as several shopping center development projects in his company, The Strawberry Group. Shahid Khan, whom I first met in 2018, also created over a billion dollars in net worth through multiple businesses. First was his automotive business, Flex-N-Gate, which manufactures and supplies large, stamped metal and welded components, assemblies, and plastic parts for the automotive industry. The second business was building the Jacksonville Jaguars—the professional football team competing in the National Football League. Khan took this team from a $760 million acquisition in 2012 to a franchise valued at more than $2 billion by *Forbes* magazine just five years later in 2017. You can bet that both of these self-made Rugged Billionaires built their empires on incredibly solid foundations; I bet you can also build a foundation and empire for yourself one day with the right attitude and acquired skills including a fervent work ethic, a humble and healthy pride, mental fortitude, and faith. The following chapters will explore these elements one by one to help you do so.

So how big is your skyscraper going to be? And how many skyscrapers do you plan to build?

CHAPTER TWO

A FERVENT WORK ETHIC

"Talent without effort is wasted talent. Effort is the one thing you can control in your life, applying that effort intelligently is next on the list."

—MARK CUBAN

THE STRONGEST AND MOST IMPORTANT FOUNDATIONAL ELEMENT for a Rugged Entrepreneur to develop is a love and respect for hard work that is so evident to the world that it is described as *fervent*. It is work performed with a burning hot intensity and energy.

Some Ruggeds establish this fervent work ethic as children helping out on a farm or in a family business, or by playing competitive sports, having a competitive job, or applying themselves competitively to academics. Others learn it later in life. As they mature and begin to realize how much opportunity has passed them by, a sense of urgency drives them to change their course. Often it is a passion or a desperate need that compels a person to work fiercely towards a goal. These experiences of hard work lead to an understanding of how greatness can be achieved by embracing challenges and working through them.

Studying the words of extremely accomplished people, you will quickly see that they don't just work hard—they also learn to apply this fervent attitude in multiple areas of their life.

Thomas Edison, the famous Rugged Entrepreneur and inventor of the light bulb among many other revolutionary devices, often credited his success to this type of work saying, *"I am glad that the eight-hour day had not been invented when I was a young man. If my life had been made up of eight-hour days, I don't believe I could have accomplished a great deal."* He was also known to say, *"I never did anything worth doing by accident, nor did any of my inventions come by accident; they came by work."* And perhaps his most famous quote on the subject was, *"Genius is one percent inspiration and ninety-nine percent perspiration."*

The legendary Green Bay Packers football coach Vince Lombardi also credited hard work for his successes, plainly acknowledging on several occasions, *"The price of success is hard work"* and quipping on another occasion, *"The only place success comes before work is the dictionary."*

Nadia Comaneci, the famous, five-time Olympic gold medalist in gymnastics and the first to earn a perfect score of 10 at the Olympic Games was heralded for making the most dangerous moves look easy in the heat of competition. Speaking of her work ethic she said, *"If I work on a move constantly, it finally doesn't seem so risky to me. The idea is that the move stays dangerous and it looks dangerous to my foes, but it is not to me. Hard work made it easy for me, and that is my secret. That is why I win."*

The great Michelangelo, who was the epitome of a Renaissance man as a sculptor, painter, architect, and poet, spoke of his work ethic saying, *"If people knew how hard I have had to work to gain my mastery, it wouldn't seem wonderful at all."*

My father, Dewey Andrew, also believes in a fervent work ethic. He grew up as a Quaker on a rugged farm in Snow Camp, North Carolina. There he learned the biblical lessons of valuing hard work and applied those lessons to academics and athletics to escape the poverty that exists beyond the basic food and shelter a farmer's life provides. The vivid memory of visiting my grandmother's uninsulated, unair-conditioned, slat-sided, wood-heated farmhouse, where she and my grandfather raised four sons together before he passed away, always impacted me profoundly. The house had only one late-addition bathroom off the main bedroom. It was there that Gramma Racheal lived self-sufficiently well into her 80s. Her grit was beyond measure. She refused to leave the farm even after she could, although she was at an age that made remaining there a challenge. What an incredibly strong woman she was and an important part of my make-up as a Rugged. If you, too, have a relative, mentor, friend, or acquaintance who has had a similar impact on you at a young age, remember and embrace those memories. They are one of the many ways you will fuel your drive. Those kinds of experiences helped shape many Ruggeds when they weren't even looking to be shaped.

On almost every one of my visits to the farm as a child, and later as an adult, I would walk on the packed dirt basketball court in the yard just beyond an incredibly old magnolia tree. There I would imagine my father as a boy on that farm. The smooth-packed dirt where he and his brothers played basketball was a good two inches lower than the surrounding dirt and grass. My father had explained to me that its surface came from countless hours of playing basketball alone or practicing with his brothers before and after doing chores and schoolwork. My young imagination reeled a movie in my head; I pictured just how much basketball it took to pack that dirt to such a deep and smooth level. This emotional word picture has stuck with me and has helped me develop and maintain a fervent work ethic. You may not have a farm history, but if you think about it, you likely have an emotional memory involving yours or someone else's inspirational climb to success through diligence and perseverance that you've committed to heart.

My father's work ethic on that dirt court and in his high school gym paid off with a scholarship to Elon College near Burlington, North Carolina. While at Elon, he met my mother, became an All American basketball player, and also directed his impressive work ethic toward his academic success. These combined achievements earned him an academic graduate scholarship at UNC Chapel Hill, where he was a working graduate assistant coach to the legendary Dean Smith. Before a short sales career and endeavoring to become a Rugged Entrepreneur himself, my father was among the first Americans drafted to play professional basketball in Italy. That country had just amended the rules of its professional league, allowing a single foreigner to play on each team. My early childhood was spent in Italy with my mother and father as part of that basketball adventure. Their intrepid spirits certainly helped shaped mine.

Growing up poor clearly motivated my father to develop his fervent work ethic. Ultimately, he became my first example of a Rugged Entrepreneur. He built multiple businesses with great success and had his own share of failures too. Today he is somewhat of a venture capitalist serving on several boards, including one of mine. His commitment to hard work keeps him busy and productive on quite a number of business projects even though he is well past the average retirement age, which, according to the 2017 Federal Reserve survey, is 59.2 for men in America. I attribute his robust mental and physical health as he approaches eighty years of age to his continued activity and to his life-long practice of being a Rugged Entrepreneur. The World Bank life expectancy data in 2016 shows U.S. males living to age 78.69, which is fifteen to eighteen years after the average retirement age. It is quite a testament that after developing a fervent work ethic as a young farm boy and applying that work ethic to school, basketball, higher education, professional basketball, sales, and a career as a Rugged Entrepreneur,

Dewey Andrew is still building "skyscrapers" twenty years longer than the average American man.

Rise and Shine

Every Rugged I have studied has a similar developmental journey where they progress from the completion of one project in life to the next, usually working on larger or more impactful projects each time. The rewards of that journey and of exercising a fervent work ethic include developing certain habits and skills, which are integral to a Rugged's life and routine. In his book *The Billion Dollar Secret*, Rafael Badziag interviewed 21 billionaires for the commonalities that led to their immense success. The book is an advanced, modern-day study of some of the world's most wealthy people. In some ways, it continues from where the great Napoleon Hill book *Think and Grow Rich* ended. In chapter seven, "The 6 Habits of Wealth," Badziag lists getting up early in the morning as the most common habit of successful entrepreneurs. He cites the average time that the self-made billionaires he interviewed chose to get up was 5:30 a.m. When I read this, I literally raised my hands in victory because I have been beating that average consistently since my late twenties. In those days I had to be up at 4:30 a.m. to be at the beverage wholesale business where I ultimately worked my way up from being the key accounts manager to being the president and part-owner. I have gotten up that early ever since. In fact, my predawn rituals are legendary among people who work in or do business with our various organizations, because that is when I send out a slew of emails, some of which are known to contain comical errors. (I admit to being grammatically challenged at times, but my thinking is always clearest at that hour!)

Actually, getting up early can be traced back even further to a time when, as a child, I was earning a small weekly allowance for doing chores. (Congratulations to parents who still teach their kids to work and earn money by completing household tasks!) By age ten, I was mowing the grass and helping to split and stack wood. I also helped my father on the weekends at his wholesale business. I learned to drive a forklift around that time, and I remember my dad explaining that we were there to unload trucks and/or rail cars that came in late on Friday so we could quickly turn product around and replenish supplies that were low or out of stock at the retail businesses we serviced by Monday afternoon. Along with a fervent work ethic, my father was customer obsessed. He did not want to wait for the weekday warehouse crew to unload the trucks because that would have delayed delivery of some of those products until Tuesday or possibly Wednesday.

Thank God that I grew up in an era when parents were not so overly protective that they kept their kids from doing challenging jobs or ones that required extra care and concentration. I developed some lifelong skills from being given those responsibilities at a young age.

In college, I always had a job and even became a small time bootlegger on the side when the drinking age changed from eighteen to nineteen, and then finally to twenty-one back in the late 1980s. I am not proud of everything I did as a young entrepreneur full of confidence, daring, and a taste for adventure, but I am not ashamed of the work ethic and ambition those days instilled in me either.

The first legitimate business I embarked on in college was one I cofounded with a fraternity brother and terrific friend, David Wilson, who was a year ahead of me at NC State. He had a great work ethic and graduated number one in his class before heading straight to graduate school. David was one of the hardest and smartest workers I had the chance to know in college. I looked up to him as someone who was focused on where he was going and how he would get there. Together we established a sales circular/newspaper entitled *College Life*. I still have a copy of the first edition. After noticing the high demand and use of coupons given away in sheets at the NC State bookstore when students bought their supplies at the start of each semester, we realized that that there was an opportunity to extend this service year-round. So we established a biweekly paper featuring coupon ads that we sold to local retailers. These ads were interwoven with stories we wrote about college life and pictures we took of students on campus. In addition to delivering stacks of papers to various student dorms and apartments, we also had them inserted in the weekly NC State newspaper twice a month.

After David got his MBA, he spent three years working for the leading consulting firm in America at that time. It was exactly the number of years he had predicted he'd work there. To no one's surprise at all, he then went on to cofound a very successful advertising company. It had always been a dream of his to do so. That company grew significantly through mergers, acquisitions, and roll-ups and was ultimately sold for $200 million. As you will read more later in this book, David has since joined me on another great business adventure. In 2019, he became an owner in bioPURE™ Services and the Chief Marketing Officer both for bioPURE™ and BoxDrop™, two companies that fall under the umbrella company named Retail Service Systems, of which I am the founder, president, and CEO.

As David got to know key people and many of the Rugged owners of our licensing and franchising businesses, he heard about my predawn routine. He asked me one day why I get up so early every day, and I told him it was a habit that had become so ingrained ever since we left NC State that it's practically a part of my DNA now. I explained that no alarm clock is ever needed. I so love being able to meditate, give thanks, and get a lot of work done in those quiet hours before and slightly after daybreak that I just wake up naturally. As someone whose only prejudice is against laziness and dishonesty, I take great pride in knowing that I'm almost always up and working at a highly productive level hours before our companies' competitors are working.

Of course, working smart is a very valuable skill to develop, too, but an entrepreneur who begins tackling the things that need to get done three to four hours earlier than everyone else, adds at least three days' worth of extra productivity to his or her weekly business construct. Those early hours are far more productive than the later hours because the phone isn't ringing and the fires of the day have not yet been lit. It is just you and your early morning routine. Your energy, primal sense of awareness, and clarity are sharper after having slept so they help generate a special kind of insight and focus. Many people who are habitual early risers say it is the rested mind that makes them so effective. Others say it's the time spent connecting to a higher level of spiritual wisdom at that hour that propels them. What I know is this: work that would generally take six to eight hours in the busy part of the day usually gets done in three to four early morning hours. On most days I firmly believe that I've already gotten a whole day ahead of my competitors before lunchtime.

It is this fervent work ethic combined with an ability to build great teams of people that have helped make one of our organizations, Retail Service Systems, one of the fastest-growing companies in America, as ranked by *Inc.* magazine.

The good news is that anyone can embrace, develop, and enjoy exercising great work habits. We all know what work is, and most of us have already tackled challenging tasks at some point in our life, so it is not a new concept. But successful entrepreneurs do not just work hard; they also have a deep sense of pride in the fact that when others notice this quality in them, they want to try it too. An excellent work ethic is truly contagious.

I said I would challenge you in this book and one of those challenges involves pushing back when others offer advice that I believe has little applicable truth in the real world. Too many people, for instance, love to say, "Find something you love, do that thing, and you will never feel as if you are actually working." Unfortunately, that statement has millions of people wasting time searching for that "thing they love" instead of learning to simply love work itself because of its productive results.

Rugged Entrepreneurs exude an aura—a visible love of work— without verbally advertising how much of it they do. They are generally very humble people. They know that there are always others who are more or less intelligent than they are and who have more or less means then they do. But they also understand that they are always in control of their own efforts and their own willingness to work as hard or harder than anyone else. In this way, work is the great equalizer and Ruggeds know that.

Game to Do What It Takes

The Ohio State University is regularly on my mind because one of the companies I founded is headquartered in Columbus, Ohio. One of the company's now-Rugged co-owners, Jerry Williams, lives there with his wife, Emily. Jerry and Emily both graduated from The Ohio State University and are wonderful examples of hard workers. They are also avid Buckeye fans. In fact, Emily is a bit of an OSU legend for being one of just three female Brutus Buckeye mascots in the school's history, and the only woman to fulfill that role during a national championship football year. Jerry and Emily are such serious fans of the school and its teams that their license plate and the name of their treasured canine companion are a nod to Woody Hayes, one of college football's greatest legends and a celebrated coach at OSU for 28 seasons, where he led the team to win 5 national titles. When Woody was once asked about his work ethic compared to the ethic of his competitors, he famously said, *"They may beat us by outcoaching me. But I resolved a long time ago that nobody would ever beat me by outworking me."*

While not an OSU graduate, I am an OSU fan because I think the school prides itself on a belief in hard work just as I do. This quote from Woody Hayes certainly indicates that. So do stories I've heard about other exceptional OSU coaches, including Urban Meyer. And, of course, graduates such as Jerry and Emily reflect this fact. I have no doubt that their fervent work ethic is an inherent part of their character, but I imagine that the school reinforced this value too. Outwardly, this ethic can be seen in the fact that Emily worked so hard to earn her masters degree, all while holding a high-level pharmaceuticals job. It can also be seen in every project for which Jerry takes responsibility. He never mentions or complains about how much work he does or how hard it is. He constantly listens to what people have to say and readily helps them with *their* work. He is the epitome of a great Rugged and corporate executive who prays for broader shoulders before praying for help from others. He doesn't have to talk about how much he works; it is evident in the results. Everyone around him sees it. We would not have founded Retail Service Systems or built BoxDrop™ so successfully without him. His humble fervent work ethic earned him equity in Retail Service Systems (RSS) and control of the BoxDrop™ wheel as its president.

This is a perfect example of how a fervent work ethic visibly spreads throughout an organization. Over time, the pride a team takes in working hard becomes part of its identity. The organization as a whole becomes even more productive. You cannot fake having a work ethic. *Hearing* someone say they have it is not the same as *seeing* that they have it.

When asked, though, Ruggeds can almost always give several examples of where their hard work, or the hard work of their team, has made a difference in a significant endeavor. Sports coaches, in particular, have a lot of insight in this area. The precise measurement of wins and losses allows them to effectively analyze the nature of success and failure. It is one reason why I love reading books such as *Leading from the Heart* by Duke University's Mike Krzyzewski (Coach K) and others. In every instance I know, these books describe a commitment to hard work in some form or fashion.

One of the more unusual books on hard work I've read was *Success Is a Choice* by Rick Pitino. Pitino is a national championship basketball coach who explained how he motivated his team to land on top. He said that he kicked off the season by telling his players that they were going to be the NCAA National Champions that year simply because they were going to be the hardest-working team in college basketball. If you are wondering how he could say with such certainty that his team would outwork other great teams, including Duke, Kansas, Kentucky,

Indiana, and Carolina, among others, his answer as offered in his book was simple: *he couldn't*. While working the team as hard as he knew how to and pushing their physical and mental boundaries anytime they practiced was certainly part of the plan, making them *believe* they were working harder than anyone else was the *key* to the plan. Instilling confidence in his players that they were indeed the hardest-working team in the league meant that they would play as if they already achieved more than anyone else; thus, they would play as if they *deserved* to win. The coach and his assistants looked for and crafted new routines that were just as hard or harder than the prior year's, and all throughout practice they constantly emphasized just how much more difficult the new challenges were. When the team ultimately won the NCAA Championship that year and the coach knew his tactic had worked, he told anyone who asked that a big part of the credit for the win went to this *belief* the team held. I happen to agree that working hard and believing that your hard work will pay off is a winning combination. Don't you? Imagine winning a National Championship at 18 to 21 years of age because you believe in the principle of hard work. How does that powerful word-picture story make you feel about your own work ethic?

Another phenomenal coach whose wisdom all Ruggeds can learn from is the late, great Pat Summitt. At the time of her retirement from coaching at the University of Tennessee in 2012, Summitt was the most-winning basketball coach in NCAA history with 1,098 career wins and 8 national championships. Her record still stands at #2 in the NCAA behind Mike Krzyzewski of Duke, who has had more than 1,100 wins and is still climbing.

Pat's coaching career was cut short due to her being diagnosed with Alzheimer's, which ultimately took her life in 2016 just four years after her final season and retirement as the Lady Vols coach. She fought her Alzheimer's battle very boldly and publicly so that her notoriety and grit could raise the kind of money and awareness that lead to a cure. This valiant effort is part of her great legacy in sports and life. Her commitment to this goal has now raised millions of dollars and impacted countless lives. In a race against time during the year before her passing, Pat partnered with the University of Tennessee Medical Center to establish a foundation in her name and to open the Pat Summitt Clinic. This remarkable facility helps comfort and treat patients with the disease and also addresses the needs of caretakers and families. All the way to the end Pat was working on something with passion. In her book, *Reach for the Summit,* she devotes an entire chapter titled "Make Hard Work Your Passion" to the benefits of this important practice. I smiled when I read that she credits her work ethic to growing up on a farm where cows don't have the luxury of taking a day off, as I know that to be true. Upon reading her book I would also credit her work ethic for her bold confidence. She tells readers that she was able to beat opponents by boldly letting them know just how she was going to do it: ***"Here's how I'm going to beat you. I'm going to outwork you. That's it. That's all there is to it."***

Ruggeds can also look to athletes, not just coaches, for wisdom on the subject of hard work. The 1991 to 1998 Chicago Bulls, led by Michael Jordan, were largely regarded as the NBA's top dynasty. They won six championships during that span and Jordan was considered by his teammates to be the hardest-working player of them all. Legendary coach Phil Jackson has written and spoken many times about Jordan's commitment to the game, sharing memories of his intense self-discipline and training habits throughout his time in the NBA. I once heard an interview with Jackson where he talked about Jordan as a rookie. He said that Jordan was known then as being a drive-and-penetrate offensive player, but not as a three-point shooter or great defensive player. Coach Jackson explained how Jordan would put in thousands of off-season hours during those early years to change that reality. In time, he developed a deadly three-point shot as well as the physicality necessary to be a great NBA defender. Jordan had built an indoor gym at his home and surprised the other team members by coming to practice without needing to warm up because he had just spent hours running drills at home. This passion to arrive already stretched, hot, and prepared to compete rubbed off on the others. Scottie Pippen asked to join Jordan for his pre-practice practice. Then more teammates gathered at Jordan's house until almost all of them were part of this extended workout too.

Jordan's much admired and fervent work ethic gave him the credibility to call teammates out when they were not playing up to team potential. The example he set as the hardest-working player enabled him to lead and expect greatness from everyone who played for the Bulls during those championship years. Coach Jackson described Jordan as humble enough to know that he had to work to be great. He also said that his willingness to put in the effort is exactly what elevated Jordan's game well above others who could have done the same but chose not to. It is no surprise to me that many athletes who adopt a fervent work ethic in sports, also apply that ethic to their business endeavors. Many of *Forbes* top-ranked athletes have turned into Rugged Billionaire entrepreneurs, including Vince McMahon, whose estimated worth is $2.2 billion; Ion Tiriac, whose estimated worth is $2 billion; and Michael Jordan, whose estimated worth is $1.7 billion.

War Stories

I learned a lot about this fervent work ethic while collaborating with and studying some of the great leaders and soldiers in the U.S. military. One of the best experiences you can possibly give yourself, as a Rugged, is time spent with members of our great armed forces. The men and women who have served and continue to serve in our military have so much to share. And for those of you reading this book who may be serving now or have served in the past, *thank you*! Having utilized our great nation's freedoms—particularly our system of capitalism and free enterprise—to build several successful businesses, I value and respect your willingness to serve and protect our country and its ideals. I view these freedoms and your service as a precious treasure.

There is a deep tradition of wartime service in my own family. Our son, Aaron, served in the Marines; my maternal grandfather was a D Day 101st Airborne paratrooper in WWII; my wife's dad, David, served in Vietnam during his thirteen years in the Army; and her sister Carol served eleven years in the Navy supporting Operation Iraqi Freedom and Operation Enduring Freedom in Afghanistan.

My enormous respect for the military has led me to spend time with WWII veterans returning to Normandy, France, where they had once stormed the beaches as young soldiers liberating an oppressed nation. I also spent time with a group of tank commanders at Fort Irwin, as well as with a reserve P-3 sub tracking squadron at Marine Corps Air Station Kaneohe Bay, among others. Daphene and I were especially fortunate to learn a lot about military leadership, work ethic, heroism, and sacrifice during a powerful talk we attended with Lt. Colonel Oliver North. While speaking with him at length one-on-one, I was impacted by many of his answers to questions I had regarding leadership development in the Corps. I will never forget his passion as he explained the intentional work regimen the military designed to train young Marines, and how strong the work ethic of those officers is as a result. He told us that he only came to a full understanding of the training's significance when he was first put in charge of young Marines during actual combat. The way he described the deep sense of personal responsibility he developed once he became accountable for the lives of these young troops really affected me and, in many ways, helped shape me as a Rugged. Being responsible for others is a very serious thing and should be recognized as such in leaders who evidence this great work ethic.

Of course, there is no comparison between the work ethic that gives a Marine officer the credibility, authority, and confidence to lead others into combat and the work ethic I owe my family, my partners, our employees, and our customers. My responsibilities, as large as they may be, could never come close to the level of responsibility military leaders bear when commanding soldiers who are putting their lives on the line for an ideal. No matter how hard I choose to work or how much weight I choose to carry, it could never match that of our great military. Knowing this humbles me and helps stoke my fervent work ethic more. Every Rugged I know hears stories and develops memories that influence them and feeds their Rugged humility in this way. If you have not, you owe it to yourself to speak with people who have served, or at the very least, read about their experiences.

My wife's fervent work ethic was equally impacted (and mine, increased) by meeting and getting to know Lieutenant Clebe McClary and his wife, Deanna. Clebe has one of the most heroic Vietnam War stories I have ever come to know. I will not share all the details of their journey here, as Clebe's book, *Living Proof*, and Deanna's book, *A Commitment to Love*, say it all so Ruggedly and beautifully. But I will offer this: Theirs is an incredibly inspiring story of how a young couple picked up the pieces of their life and marriage after his body was shattered beyond recognition by the weaponry of war. Through an extraordinary work ethic and a tremendous faith, they emerged stronger. Together they have transcended into a life of helping others. Whereas 80 percent of relationships affected by such extensive wartime injury end in immediate divorce, this couple persevered. Deanna's book, in particular, has broadened Daphene's and my outlook on what work, sacrifice, and commitment mean in a relationship. Daff has always believed in working hard as a wife and business partner. She would tell you herself that being raised by a single mom until age ten and having a humble and often poor early childhood are what inspired her to work passionately for what is important in life. But she will also tell you that Deanna's story has anchored her belief in determined partnership that much more.

People love to throw around statements like, "You should respect me more," but often, they don't earn the respect they are looking for. Love is given, respect is earned, and my wife has earned all the respect I could possibly have for a person, and then some, with her steadfast commitment to our relationship, family, and business interests. Daff and I have often said that we hoped our work ethic, success, and example would inspire others to make similar commitments. We see the skyscrapers we are building and our life together as a book we continue to write with each passing day. We keep an old, handmade, leather-bound book about six inches thick of blank pages on a desk in one of my offices. That book is a constant reminder that our next chapter is yet to be written. It is up to us to go out and live a life that reads like a grand novel, full of many creative, formative, and purposeful adventures. We hope our example entices others to have such adventures too.

While athletes and soldiers have many inspiring war stories to tell, entrepreneurs have a type of war story all their own. They're what I call "Rugged War Stories" and just like the other war stories we've heard, they are a byproduct of having a fervent work ethic too. They are experiences that ultimately become valuable tools for building a Rugged culture within an organization. Before I explain what they are and how a Rugged can identify and apply them in their own journey, let me share with you what prompted the concept and solidified the name in my mind.

Years ago, I had the opportunity to observe a ten-day exercise aboard the *John C. Stennis*, a Nimitz-class nuclear aircraft carrier. During that stretch of time, I met an amazing group of fighter pilots and team members in Marine Fighter Attack Squadron 323, also known as VMFA 323 or the "Come to Fight, Come to Win" Death Rattlers. The days spent with the Death Rattlers in their "Ready Room" onboard that powerful warship were humbling beyond belief and led me later to do my own deep dive into the specifics of how Marines build culture.

At that time, I was curious about the ways the military transforms young people into strong men and women and compels such amazing acts of heroism from them. What I discovered is a tradition of story-telling that contributes to the ongoing Lore of The Corps. From the time Marines begin boot camp, the Corps puts them through arduous trans-formational regimens that push their physical and mental boundaries. At the same time, these recruits learn all about the feats of the Marines who came before them. These stories about their predecessors are incredibly powerful and inspirational. They convey a sense of history and instill pride in being part of the Marine culture.

During boot camp, a Marine recruit is intentionally called "recruit" because being called "Marine" is an honor, and recruits have not yet earned that honor. That becomes very clear as the recruits hear these stories. Only after completing the grueling twelve-week training and passing the fifty-four-hour test of their mental and physical toughness, known as The Crucible, will a recruit be called a Marine. By then a Marine knows he or she is part of a brotherhood/sisterhood. These war stories are clearly a crucial and intentional component in building the kind of work ethic and pride Marines are known for all around the world. It is in no small measure what leads them through The Crucible, and so often, what leads them through battle.

Understanding how potent war stories can be, I decided to implement a program using "Rugged War Stories" in our organizations too. The concept alone empowers team members, motivates them to meet and surpass goals, fosters a culture of hard work and healthy pride, and, of course, yields plenty of long-term success.

Rugged Lore

Rugged War Stories in our organizations are typically centered on extraordinary accomplishments—instances when someone went the extra mile or made a truly commendable effort. Recognizing and talking about these endeavors, risks, and victories can help you create your own corporate lore. During Retail Service Systems' first year of building the model for what is now the BoxDrop™ franchising operation, a furniture manufacturer in Haleyville, Alabama, abruptly announced that they would no longer be shipping products west of the Mississippi as they were planning on closing their business. Unfortunately, two of our customers who regularly carried these goods would have been negatively impacted by this closure. They had placed back-to-school ads promoting these products before they knew they would no longer be available. Both customers had also prepaid for their orders. One customer was in Colorado Springs, Colorado, and the other was in Chico, California. When we spoke to the manufacturer to see what our options were, we were told that if we wanted the furnishings at all, we had to pick them up within the next two days. Our COO at the time, Jerry Williams, was a logistics whiz with a logistics degree from The Ohio State University, so it would not have been difficult for him to hire an LTL carrier (a transport vehicle for less than a full truckload) to make the trip. Instead, my wife, Daphene, saw this as an opportunity to add to our company lore and suggested that we resolve the issue ourselves. She proposed that we embark on this adventure with the intention of creating our own Rugged War Story.

With only a two-day notice, we rented a twenty-seven-foot Penske box truck out of Greenville, South Carolina, and spent the next three days on the road. First, we drove to that starting point in Haleyville, Alabama, to pick up the two orders, which barely fit in the truck. After loading up all of the goods, we then headed several thousand miles across the country to personally deliver them to our customers. It was a tough, nonstop haul. While war stories often involve heroism, they can also involve a bit of humor, even if the circumstances don't seem all that funny at the time. It's usually in retelling the details of your adventure that you discover just how hilarious it was. As it happened, we had humorous *and* harrowing moments on our trip.

We actually surprised the Rugged franchisee on our first stop. This customer knew we had arranged for delivery, but he hardly expected it would be *me and my wife* making the drop-off. After a good laugh, we unloaded the furniture, said our good-byes, and continued north towards the Colorado-Wyoming state line. It was there that we were detained at a weigh station. After inspecting our truck and its half load of boxed furniture, the DMV officer said we had to have a CDL (Commercial Drivers License) to be making such a delivery. She then proceeded to explain the process for impounding the truck and the goods until we could pay a fine and get the proper permit to drive into Wyoming.

We were only about 400 yards across the state line and had made it almost two-thirds of the way to our final destination before hitting this snag. Fortunately, we looked as if we had been on the road for quite some time. I was unshaven and hadn't showered since we left. A burly truck driver overhearing the discussion sympathized and came to our rescue saying, "They're hauling furniture they own, so they're not contract drivers. They're just moving." Thank God for his quick thinking. We were so happy to be supported by someone who knew the rules. That opened the door for me to explain that we were, in fact, moving furniture we owned to a new location and that this was the one and only time they would ever see me driving a truck across their state line. Thanks to how pathetic we must have looked and to the bold trucker who interjected, the officer from the DMV let us go on our way. This reminded me of the Coleman Cox quote, *"I am a great believer in luck; the harder I work the more of it I seem to have."*

When we arrived at our second stop in Chico, California, our Rugged franchisee didn't recognize me because I had practically grown a full beard by then! He wouldn't even let me in his doorway at first because I didn't have a dock appointment to deliver to his store. Imagine his surprise when I identified myself! It still makes us laugh to this day.

Our willingness to work that hard to ensure our customers' success really made an impression. Just as you might expect, the story of our extra-mile effort made the rounds. RSS officially had a first-year Rugged War Story. It is now part of the lore of our company and has spawned many other acts of fortitude and perseverance throughout our organization. When you create war stories around your and others' exemplary work ethics, that code of conduct spreads to your leaders and your teams until it ultimately defines the whole company's work ethic. This is how a culture of hard work and healthy pride is established.

Adding to your treasure trove of war stories can be an awesome and fun adventure—one that allows you to be very creative. Personally driving a truck across country, surprising our franchisees, presenting a solution to their #1 problem at the time, and somehow dodging impoundment at the weigh station is a great war story, but it's not the funniest or most committed war story I have to tell!

When I was the thirty-two-year-old general manager, president, and minority owner in a wholesale beer and soft-drink distributorship, I also owned a rodeo production company that held PRCA rodeos and bull-riding events. In the hopes of creating a company war story that might also drive sales, I engineered a bull-riding event sponsored by Coors and Dodge that built upon another sales promotion already in the works. We were slated to sell Coors 18-packs at a discount for the sixty days leading up to the main Saturday bull-riding event. Each 18-pack in the market contained a coupon for a half-price ticket to the event. To incentivize our sales team to get even more 18-packs out there, I proposed that if our company sales were up 100 percent on Coors Original during those two months, I would ride a bull in the main lineup alongside all of the cowboys. My team was either very committed to the event and their sales success or they were very committed to seeing me dead, because sales over that two-month period were up over 120 percent! My challenge had worked . . .but now I had to cowboy up.

A deal is a deal, and I strongly believe that you have to honor your word, so that night, I had to ride a bull, like it or not. We love to create Rugged Entrepreneur shirts to give to our entrepreneur customers on special occasions. The shirts feature Rugged statements on the back. One of my favorites has always been, *"If you climb in the saddle, be ready for the ride."* The night of that rodeo, I suited up with this motto in mind and entered the main lineup just like every other cowboy riding in the event. I drew a Brahma bull with a big hump on his back and short sawed horns. As I stood at the chute with my vest, number, and chaps on tight, Daphene was there beside me crying her eyes out. The rider who had preceded me was injured in a bad fall and stomp. When they called my name, I climbed to the top of the chute. My heart was pounding so fast that I felt like it would explode out of my chest. At that very moment I wondered what the heck I had done. *Why did I create this event? This whole promotion? This crazy sales contest?* War stories can evolve in so many different ways because a true Rugged Entrepreneur possesses a wealth of business creativity and is typically very adventuresome, yet in that moment I couldn't exactly remember how this one began. Nor could I imagine how it would end.

As I threw my leg over the bull's hump and started lowering myself onto that angry beast's back, he rocked, snorted, and banged from side to side against the chute walls. I was not only in way over my head, I was fully convinced that my life was in danger. The cowboy spotters helped strap in my left hand and before I knew it, I was firmly sitting on top of this fourteen-hundred-pound animal, scared out of my mind. It was less than a second before they asked me if I was good to go. I looked down at my grip, then back up at them and said yes. The buzzer sounded and I all I heard was the gate clanking open. That bull lunged forward instantly, nearly ripping my arm out of its socket and tearing the back of my shirt from shoulder to shoulder. I weathered that first leap, but I also slid to the back of the bull's haunches, which is the equivalent of a launch pad. The next thing I knew, my feet were in the air out in front of me and I was hoping that I'd somehow land running. Instead, my butt took the fall. That monster had thrown me about four feet high and about three feet in front of his crazy eyes and threatening horns. My one and only famous bull ride lasted all of two seconds. Thank God for the clowns because, before I could piece together what had happened, one of them helped me up and sent me heading for safety, while the other two distracted the bull. I had a heck of a night and a heck of a bruise on each of my butt cheeks the next day. But I also had a heck of a war story.

After holding that contest and showcasing my bull-riding skills (or lack of them), our company embraced a Rugged cowboy spirit. We had a real get-it-done attitude. We created various cowboy-themed shirts and gave them out to all of our employees throughout the year. The pride around our achievement and our creativity grew. We also saw an immense spike in sales for Original Coors. We were soon known among fellow distributors nationwide for our "cowboy flare" and for our remarkable increase in business. I was asked to be on the Coors Mid Atlantic Advisory Board and was also elected to the North Carolina Wholesalers board. In both instances, I was the youngest member. We booked a subsequent bull-riding event the next year, where I topped the previous year's bull ride by proposing marriage in the middle of the arena to my awesome and very surprised then-girlfriend, Daphene. We told her that she would be giving away a guitar autographed by a well-known country singer to keep her from getting suspicious. When she came out with the guitar in hand, I dropped to one knee and popped the question.

Those two war stories changed the culture of an entire organization, got me on a few prestigious boards, broadened my contacts with other successful Ruggeds, and, most importantly, helped me land my wife. War stories can lead to great things for you and your organization. They can take a day, a week, a month, or even several years to unfold, but once completed and visibly associated with a successful outcome, war stories live on for decades. In addition to inspiring your own organization's members, they're often recounted in other organizations too. The return on investment is great, and every new war story sparks the potential for another to exist soon after. All of that said, I don't suggest that you ride a bull to get a war story on record. But I do guarantee that every Rugged already has (or will have) their own personal equivalent to that bull ride in their career. What is yours?

Whether you are well into life as a Rugged Entrepreneur or you are just looking to make the leap, war stories require that you have a fervent work ethic to help you get through them. Each personal war story impacts you as much as it impacts the business you are currently building. They form the foundation of who you are, how others perceive you, and how your presence—both mentally and physically—make any team you are part of better. All Rugged Entrepreneurs have war stories. I don't know a single Rugged who hasn't had at least one out-of-the-ordinary experience. In fact, most of the Ruggeds I know have conquered many exciting challenges like the ones above and have also overcome many difficult and trying ones too.

In my early thirties, when the Internet was exploding with entrepreneurial opportunities and Amazon was just a fledgling online bookstore, I found myself facing one of those difficult kinds of challenges—one that really tested my mettle as a Rugged. I guess you could say that Daphene and I saw the future and really wanted to get in on the game by starting a B2B Internet business. I had already founded a real estate company and a rodeo production company; I was the president and general manager of a multimillion-dollar beverage wholesale business; and I also owned 30 percent of that beverage company. I was sure I could make something of this new venture too. The challenge arose when the 70 percent owner and CEO of the beverage wholesale company came to me with an ultimatum. He reminded me that I ran the business day-to-day and that I was drawing a strong compensation package in excess of $200,000 per year. He was concerned that my having yet another business would divide my attentions and potentially harm his bottom line. In a face-to-face meeting he told me that I had to choose between my new Internet business or his distribution business. Although there was a chance that I would someday own the entire beverage wholesale company, at the time I was being forced to choose something he controlled more than I did.

Being smaller than all but one student in my graduating high school class, I developed a fighter's spirit, which only grew along with my height during my boxing days in college. I had a scrappy nature and especially hated the feeling of having someone's thumb on me, so I made my decision to resign on the spot. Driving home from that meeting, I called Daphene wondering if I had made a mistake. I will never forget her reassuring words at that moment. She told me that she was excited we would now be in control of our own destiny and that we should attack that destiny with everything we had. She knew that would mean some big sacrifices, but she also knew we had the work ethic to make a success of anything we set our minds to.

In making that choice, I immediately lost three quarters of my very solid income. Beyond downsizing, we had to find a way to make up some of the shortfall so we could live and still be able to invest in our fledgling business. To close that income gap while leaving the whole day and night open on Tuesdays, Thursdays, Saturdays, and Sundays, and at least the evenings on Mondays and Wednesdays for the new business, I had to get pretty creative. I immediately got a *USA Today* paper route because of the flexibility it presented. I picked up the papers in a Winn-Dixie grocery store parking lot at 4:30 a.m., then spent the next three hours running the route. *USA Today* was only delivered Monday through Friday in those days so the early morning delivery hours left me free to build the new business in the remaining day and evening hours. At the same time, I talked to a friend who owned a small construction company and told him that I wanted to learn some carpentry skills. I promised I'd be great at helping him for minimal pay. I worked three days a week from 8:00 a.m. until 1:00 p.m. on a test basis at first. A Rugged's willingness to work fuels his or her ability to solve even the most dramatic problems. A lot of people try to wait or look for what they call the "optimal" solution, letting valuable income-earning time slip by. Ruggeds create solutions by going after what's in front of them while working on their larger goal, and then rearranging factors as needed along the way. Ruggeds typically say things such as, "I'm getting this done now and will figure out a better way while moving forward."

Even though Daphene had not worked full time as a flight attendant for several years because our prior business ventures supported us well, she stepped up to help during that time by returning full time to the airlines while I worked the other two part-time jobs. When she wasn't away on a trip, she often ran the paper route with me. I fondly remember the singing game we made up to pass the time. In addition to juggling these jobs, we both committed every waking hour to building our Internet business. We made the work fun and something to be proud of. We laughed a lot and developed an ever-greater respect for each other and for our shared willingness to do whatever needed to be done.

I have never known a man or woman who matches my wife Daphene's fervent work ethic and desire to make the things she is responsible for better. I was not always great at building incredible relationships and have had to learn a lot about doing that right from her. Beyond love or passion, a great marriage and a great business relationship benefit immensely from an evident level of mutual respect. My wife's work ethic has earned that respect and credibility from me and all who know her. People often comment on what amazing partners we are, and I must say that it is this appreciation and esteem for each other that make this true. Our relationship is one of my secret weapons. (And now that I'm writing about it so publicly, it's my not-so-secret weapon.) When two Ruggeds join forces in business and in marriage, one plus one no longer equals two. In that equation, the two digits sit side by side and what you get is an eleven—a value more than five times greater than two! I love that visual picture, don't you? It makes it so easy to remember the power of love and partnership.

I've gathered all of these personal, sports, military, and business stories to help you understand why building a fervent work ethic is such an essential part of a Rugged Entrepreneur's foundation. Beyond the physical productivity it creates, a solid work ethic has a psychological component that cannot be ignored. In addition to impacting the organization's culture, it also builds an individual's sense of *merito*. This Latin word refers to the state of knowing deep inside that one deserves success. Sometimes I use another word I concocted instead of *merito* because I think its meaning is clearer. That word is "deservance." When you believe you deserve to win or succeed, it affects everything you do. It impacts your psyche, your confidence, your expectations, your actions, your communications, your relationships, and ultimately, your results. To be clear, deservance is *not* entitlement. Deservance is knowing that you warrant success and therefore are willing to *work* for it. There is *no* expectation that success will be dropped in your lap without you earning it. The coach and all those players on the NCAA champion team I mentioned earlier certainly had a sense of deservance, but they also had the mental and physical calluses, scrapes, bruises, and bumps to prove that they earned their success.

Rugged Entrepreneur billionaires from Sam Walton and Bill Gates to Mark Cuban and Jeff Bezos, all have stories to share about their legendary work ethics. So do many others from all over the world whose names may be less familiar to you. One of the most influential Rugged Entrepreneurs in Asia, for instance, is Li Ka-shing. In 2018, he was ranked as the 30th-richest person on the planet with an estimated worth of $31 billion. To help you visualize that amount of wealth, let's take a second to draw a distinction between a million dollars and a billion dollars. A million dollars stacked in hundred-dollar bills would stand a little less than two feet high. A billion dollars stacked up in hundred-dollar bills would stand one hundred feet higher than the Washington Monument. Li Ka-shing's net worth is equivalent to *thirty-one* of those billion-dollar stacks.

Li Ka-shing is the epitome of a self-made man. His father died of tuberculosis when Li was just fourteen years old. But even before then, Li had to quit school and get a job in a plastics factory, working sixteen hours a day, to support his family. He started at the lowest rung of child labor and worked his way up, learning every task from cleaning to machine maintenance. He ultimately earned an opportunity to work in sales. When he applied the same fervent work ethic that enabled him to endure sixteen-hour workdays as a laborer to his sales efforts, he became a dominant force in that area too. By age nineteen, he was promoted to general manager of the business, overseeing several hundred employees. A few years later he started his own plastics company. To ensure its success, he wore every hat necessary at first. (That's a Rugged trait.) Ultimately, his fervent work ethic and bottom-to-top, experienced-based wisdom enabled him to build that company and rise not just to millionaire status, but to multi-BILLIONAIRE status.

I have no doubt that Li Ka-shing understands the concept of *merito* or deservance and that it, along with his fervent work ethic, drove his business success. Do you?

When a person doesn't believe that they deserve to win or succeed, they usually don't. A sense of deservance magnifies success. It extends from an individual to his or her teams, customers, suppliers, and beyond. It literally permeates the entire culture of the business and the cultures of those who associate with it. Soon everyone within your radius believes that success is possible and deserved and strives harder to attain it. The legend of yours and your team's work ethic becomes an advertisement for your organization. This advertisement reveals the organization's DNA—the story of who you are collectively. In today's world of exponential social connections, the impact of that advertised DNA is far more valuable than ever before. It is now one of the cornerstones of successful Rugged Entrepreneurialism.

By the way, remember the RSS Rugged war story I told earlier, about how Daff and I drove a truck cross-country to personally deliver goods to two franchisees that needed those goods? Well, that effort yielded some amazing developments. The owner-operator franchisees we made deliveries to in that rented yellow Penske truck on that trip have since become two of our most important national leaders. Brad Loy is BoxDrop™'s Chief Coaching Officer and the man charged with creating and continuously improving our business coaching programs while literally coaching BoxDrop™'s coaches. And Bob Wert became one of our stellar Division Business Coaches and the developer and overseer of our BoxDrop™ Sofa program as its National Director. Both are phenomenal Rugged Entrepreneurs who have owned and built very successful RSS franchises. Do you suppose that Daff's and my work ethic and willingness to build that war story had anything to do with attracting highly successful Rugged Entrepreneurs such as Brad and Bob to become part of our National Leadership Team? Do you think it may have enticed them in any way to become an excited part of our incredible journey? Daphene and I certainly do. We always marvel at how we've been able to attract great people such as Brad and Bob to the teams we build. We strongly believe one of the main reasons for this phenomenon is that our fervent work ethic draws them to us and to our mission. We always build great teams because we deserve to have great people on them. We earned that right as Ruggeds, and you can too.

Before closing this chapter about the most important component in building a Rugged foundation, I ask you to take some time to process what you've read so far about a Rugged's fervent work ethic. Do any emotional word pictures come to mind? Again, these are images, words, or stories that you instantly associate with a particular message to help you easily remember that message. Solidifying what you have discovered in each chapter will help your findings stay with you as you move forward in building your own Rugged foundation.

Here's one more image for you: A Rugged exudes a bold attitude and a pattern of taking action that shouts to the whole world, "Bring it on. *I'm not afraid of the work.* I'm Rugged. I can shoulder the weight of what I'm building, even as I add new levels to my business. I face difficult challenges and trade war stories about them later. I deserve success, and I won't ever apologize for being a winner."

That, my friend, is the mindset you must develop and embrace to be a Rugged. It will empower you to build lore, to build teams, to build culture, to build your own wisdom of deservance, and to build businesses that stand tall in the marketplace like the skyscrapers they are. Have you learned to love and embrace work yet? Hard work? Physical work? Complex mental work? Work takes lots of different forms and a Rugged Entrepreneur embraces all of them to have a work ethic described as being "*fervent.*"

CHAPTER THREE

A HUMBLE AND HEALTHY PRIDE

"If you compare yourself to others, you may become vain and bitter; for always there will be greater and lesser persons than yourself."
—From the poem "If" by Rudyard Kipling

To succeed as an entrepreneur in a demanding business environment, you must be hungry for knowledge. All entrepreneurs are aware that there is always something more they could learn to improve their business, and it's safe to say that those who have fallen short of their goals are especially aware of that fact. Frequently, they'll look to expand their knowledge in the area of their business *expertise*. They will take more accounting, marketing, or finance courses or read up on industry specifics. But building long-term, highly successful Rugged organizations requires a lot more than that. It requires broadening your knowledge to many other areas that are not so business-centric. Rugged Entrepreneurs have a voracious appetite for developing and improving their business acumen, but they also have a desire, ability, and willingness to push the boundaries of their knowledge. This is how one ultimately leads with wisdom.

Thomas Corley and Dave Ramsey are well known for their research into the behaviors that lead to financial success. Both Tom's book *Rich Habits* and Dave's book *The Total Money Makeover* explore the practices that contribute to a millionaire's success. Their studies show that becoming an avid reader is one of the key habits almost all millionaires develop. In today's world, where the Internet, e-books, podcasts, and YouTube videos provide more affordable access to information than at any other time in history, this is a habit that *anyone* can develop. Information on almost any topic you could possibly want to learn about is available to us all. Because of that, developing expertise on any subject is fairly simple. All you have to do is be willing to put a small effort towards that goal.

All entrepreneurs should develop this habit. But you should know there is more to wisdom than just reading books or informational access learning (aka, googling). Ruggeds are able to successfully bridge the massive chasm between business expertise and true business wisdom by exercising what I call "Rugged Intellect." There is a mental state or place where one is able to access a *universal* wisdom that is vastly beyond measure. From that place, a Rugged is able to grow their business wisdom exponentially because they have liberated themselves to a higher and broader way of learning. Most people are unaware how big the gap between business expertise and universal wisdom is. Business expertise is having specific knowledge or skills, while universal wisdom is having deeper, more expansive abilities to judge, discern, and perceive what presently exists and what is possible. It taps into your own experiences and accumulated knowledge for guidance as well as into the comprehensive body of knowledge the universe collects from us all.

Let me tell you about a mental exercise I engaged in to help you get a handle on what universal wisdom is. I was recently on a trip with two business partners in our bioPURE™ Services adventure. One of my travel companions was Brandon Kinder, a young Rugged Entrepreneur I like to describe as "rare air." Brandon is the President of bioPURE™. The other companion was Jim Wilson, bioPURE™'s CEO. We were heading to a very important meeting with a chemical manufacturer. Each of us was aware that we needed great results from this meeting. We had three corporate bioPURE™ locations in operation and one pioneer franchise about to open soon. The main location, built by Brandon, a very pure Rugged Entrepreneur, had reached a six-figure income in its first few years assuring us that its service fulfilled an important need in the marketplace. His work ethic was such that he built that original business while maintaining a full-time job and while he and his wife were raising four small children. We all believed we had a scalable home run on our hands, but before we could expand further, we needed to get our manufacturing and supply chain operation working optimally so we could unleash a national program and support the explosive growth we anticipated. The mission in the meeting we were heading to was to solve whatever sourcing challenges we were running up against now and avert any such challenges in the future as we expanded operations.

Jim Wilson was at the wheel of the car that day. He is one of the smartest men I know, and he has been a friend since the fifth grade. Both of his sons are Rugged Entrepreneurs in the Retail Service Systems family of businesses as well. Jim cut his teeth in corporate America after graduating from the University of Tennessee and going to work for Raytheon in their missiles program. While doing that, he was also earning his masters degree in business at East Tennessee State University in Johnson City. Upon graduating with that MBA, he joined Eastman Chemical, a multibillion-dollar company headquartered in Kingsport, where he spent the next twenty-seven years. During that time, Jim rapidly climbed up the corporate ladder, and on the side, he and I worked together to Ruggedly build the very successful B2B Internet business I mentioned previously. Jim ultimately became the Director of

Global Procurement for Eastman and was responsible for sourcing raw materials for plants all over the world. His specialized expertise in the chemical business and in sourcing have been invaluable to our BoxDrop™ furniture organization and to bioPURE™ Services, where he is an owner, its CEO, and a Rugged Entrepreneur.

Naturally, Jim's knowledge in the chemical industry and his instincts as a Rugged made him the perfect person to set up and lead this meeting with Brandon, myself, and the chemical company we were visiting that day. As we were leaving the city of Greenville, South Carolina, and heading toward our destination in Alabama, Brandon, who has a keen mind, asked questions that opened up an opportunity for a coaching moment about "universal wisdom" and how to tap into it. The lesson began with me asking them if they realized how fast Greenville was growing. They both immediately answered yes and then some discussion ensued about how exponential the growth actually was. Soon thereafter, I asked them, "As we leave this booming city and head to Alabama, if a tragic car accident takes your life, Brandon, will that have a horrific impact on your young family?" It was meant to be a provocative and shocking question and Brandon instantly said, "Absolutely."

I quickly pivoted and said, "Did you know there are more than a billion people in China?" Brandon did know that and answered yes. I then asked him, "As horrific as your death would be to your family, how many of those billion people in China would even know about it?" Brandon's answer was exactly what I thought it would be, "None." I explained that there are another half a billion just in India and almost seven and a half billion people on the entire planet. That example illustrates just how insignificant we are in the larger scope of things. It is a humbling truth, but it also provides a sense of the vast numbers of others who exist in our universe. I told Brandon that understanding our significance in the scope of more than seven billion people was an important exercise necessary to establish humility—the number one requirement to open the mental doors to universal wisdom.

I then pointed to a large pine tree we could see on the side of the highway and asked, "Do you think there are more than one hundred different facts about that pine tree regarding its chemical makeup, root system, needle structure and purpose, growth processes, seeding, and so forth that one could explore?" Brandon said that it sure seemed like there must be. I then proceeded to ask if we could say the same about the oaks and the dogwoods as well as the wildflowers and grass in the median. Next, I turned to Jim to inquire about how many different types of engineers there were in the city we just exited, as Jim's background is in engineering. He thought probably every type was located there, from civil, mechanical, and chemical to electrical and structural engineers as well as a myriad of other specialists in the middle. I asked him about how many elements of expertise existed in the minds of all those engineers in Greenville. He answered the number would likely be too vast to say. We then discussed the thought of how much wisdom existed in every professional's mind from doctors and accountants to entrepreneurs in just the city of Greenville. We asked ourselves, "If we looked at each element of knowledge as a molecule in the universe of wisdom, how many would there be in the minds of Greenville residents only?" Taking the exercise a step further, we wondered about how many molecules of knowledge and facts there are in our solar system outside of Earth's atmosphere, to infinity and beyond. You see where this was going. In no time at all we concluded that the scope of the universe's wisdom is unfathomable. That exercise illustrates the incalculable amount of information that exists. It should humble you to think that God's gift to you is to be "full of wisdom." It should also intrigue you to want to become more capable of tapping into it. I finished that exercise with Brandon and Jim explaining that only by being humble enough to see and understand how little wisdom we possess individually in comparison to the collective body of wisdom seven billion people hold can we begin to access that universal wisdom.

Having humility is the key to unlocking the flow of universal wisdom. That exchange between you and the universe is what I call "Rugged Intellect." Rugged Intellect allows us to access and absorb portions of the experience and knowledge that are all around us on such a deep level that they lead to the attainment of street sense, common sense, and expert sense all in one channel of our mind. Numerous authors since Napoleon Hill published his book *Think and Grow Rich* have addressed this access to what I am calling universal wisdom. Hill discusses it as tapping into a "sixth sense" and accessing "invisible counselors" who literally speak to you.

For me, Rugged Intellect lends one a sense of discernment into the inner workings of people, teams, processes, and long-term strategic thinking that most people never develop. The Rugged Intellect is crucial to having vision, being able to problem-solve effectively, executing short- and long-term strategic planning, and so much more. It is essential for the kind of dynamic team building that enables an organization to stay ahead of the changing atmospheres in which they, their people, and teams operate.

Access to information and wisdom is on the Internet and in books for those who want to succeed in business, but all the access in the world is irrelevant if someone is not teachable and coachable at the highest levels of learning. To be a Rugged you must *"dare to be wise"* or **sapere aude,** as the saying goes in Latin. You must cultivate Rugged Intellect.

In My Humble Opinion

In the same way that humility is the key to unlocking universal wisdom, there is one personality trait that will bar access to such wisdom in an instant. Throughout all my years of studying both success and failure in business, learning what *not* to do or how *not* to be is often as important as learning what to do or how to be. I have seen plenty of fervently hard-working entrepreneurs who hungered for and cultivated a specific business expertise ultimately fail to become the Rugged they aspired to be simply because they had a problematic ego. If only they could see what their self-aggrandizing behavior was costing them. It literally pains me to see how silly their overinflated egos can make them look, and how much it hinders their ability to become someone who is so much more productive than they are. There is a word for such people, and that word is *navel-gazer*.

I've always felt that the emotional word picture *navel-gazer* creates in your mind should be enough to deter you from being one too. But if you feel the word applies to you—either a little or a lot—don't fret. A navel-gazer doesn't have to stay that way for long. All one has to do is embrace the quality of humility. Interestingly enough, according to the Merriam-Webster dictionary, the literal definition of humility is "a state of freedom from arrogance." Think about that for a moment. FREEDOM from arrogance. Who wants their freedom to be taken away by anything, let alone by something they have the power to control? Imprisonment or losing your freedom to your own ego is foolish and creates a myriad of unnecessary challenges. While the expression *navel-gazer* needs no explanation, it means the excessive contemplation of oneself at the expense of a **wider view.** A Rugged engaged in his or her *Sapere aude* challenge learns to use their Rugged Intellect to access the *wider view* the universe offers. Here are the many ways navel-gazers block that view versus how a Rugged seeks it:

Navel-gazers don't maximize teamwork effectiveness. Ruggeds DO!

By nature, a navel-gazer has an insatiable need for attention. His or her ego is so inflated it conflicts with teamwork because it sucks most of the oxygen from the environment. No one else can breathe, think, or contribute in the presence of a navel-gazer. Team building is discussed throughout this book in great detail because it is a skill all Ruggeds develop to the highest level. As Steve Jobs, the founder of Apple, once said, *"Great things in business are never done by one person; they're done by a team of people."* A Rugged learns that they must create teams and organizational cultures where the focus revolves around the purpose and goal of their shared mission. Bringing people together and contributing on equal grounds of mutual respect is essential to creating that atmosphere.

Navel-gazers tend to believe that the culture of a team should revolve around them. Thus, they easily feel in competition with the leader, or just as bad, they vie for his or her attention, disrupting the team's mission and purpose. A team's purpose should always be a unifying factor. Everyone should have respect for the other team members and a healthy pride in seeing their mission through to completion. Because Ruggeds possess Rugged Intellect, they are great team players who not only shine within the team, they promote and elevate the contributions of others, raising the entire team's unity and productivity. Ruggeds build teams that play to win. Navel-gazers build teams that play hoping not to make mistakes.

Navel-gazers don't have a thankful nature. Ruggeds DO!

A very wise book that has been around for centuries teaches people to give thanks in all things. Ruggeds appreciate the world and are continually building upon or improving what has already been built before them. They recognize that there is wisdom to be found both in successes and failures, and that helps them persevere in building a better future. Ruggeds are thankful for all of it—the good and the bad, the tough and the easy, the right and the wrong, the ups and the downs. No one is *born* thankful. As they develop wisdom, Ruggeds learn that gratitude is a necessity. Navel-gazers, on the other hand, believe they are superior to others and often possess a type of entitlement complex that expects others to comply with them because their way must be the right way. Navel-gazers wear a comparative set of glasses; whenever they look at others, they measure themselves against those others and get very frustrated when another person's way is perceived as better, different, or even equal to their own.

Navel-gazers almost never admit to having faults and tend to be very defensive if someone suggests otherwise. They avoid accepting responsibility for mistakes, usually finding others to lay the blame on. Blaming others, as opposed to assuming personal responsibility, leads navel-gazers to disregard and be ungrateful for the views and opinions of other contributors. As a result, they generally find positions where they operate alone or somewhat in the dark. A navel-gazer's lack of thankfulness drives people away, whereas a Rugged's appreciative spirit attracts people to them. There is tremendous wisdom in being thankful. It enhances a Rugged's ability to build great teams and retain talent. Of all the Ruggeds I have been blessed to know, by far the most thankful of them has been Kelly Harris.

When she began working part-time for extra money as an appointment setter for a Rugged Entrepreneur named Brad Loy, Kelly was a single mother of four who was also waitressing to make ends meet. She is ambitious yet very humble. She is also teachable *and* coachable. In time, she moved up, working in sales for that Rugged Entrepreneur, and her thankfulness and coach-ability continued to help her develop a Rugged Intellect. When the opportunity came for her to buy that business, she was ready. She shaped herself into a Rugged Entrepreneur who not only became the largest dealer in a national chain of over 400 licensed dealers and franchisees, she was also the favorite customer of the licensor/franchisor's customer service team. She passionately offers her time and wisdom as a coach in the organization. It is as if she is on a "thankful mission" to give back and empower other entrepreneurs. One day, another Rugged Entrepreneur, who owned his own construction business, noticed this wonderful quality in Kelly. She happened to be selling this fellow, named Trent Harris, a large sectional sofa when he saw in her a kindred spirit he couldn't resist. Today Kelly and Trent are building a huge business together and have since added a fifth child to the Harris family. They keep that now famous sectional sofa Trent purchased from Kelly in their family room as a Harris family war story memento.

I have observed a good number of navel-gazers who had access to everything Kelly did, including Kelly's very own direct coaching wisdom. Foolishly, they brushed their access to those gifts aside because they were ego blind to the gifts' value—and worse, they were ego blind to their own need to learn! Their inability to become humble is exactly what keeps them from being teachable. When you lack teachability you lack humility. When you lack humility, you are throwing away the key that unlocks the doorway to universal wisdom. Sadly, because navel-gazers credit themselves for almost everything, they lack gratitude for much of anything, and they never become the Rugged they are capable of being.

Navel-gazers don't control their temper well.
Ruggeds DO!

Pay close attention to the word "control" here. I am not suggesting that Ruggeds don't have a temper or that they don't get angry. All Ruggeds get irritated and many, like me, have what I describe as a passionate temper. But unlike navel-gazers, Ruggeds develop the emotional wisdom to harness and control their frustrations. They have learned ways to cultivate and channel that energy, often directing its fuel toward something productive. They also use that passion when making important points to others, as fiery speech is not easily forgotten. Navel-gazers lack the emotional wisdom and maturity to harness their temper in such highly productive ways. They wield their anger either uncontrollably or as a weapon, attempting to manipulate or belittle others to get what their entitled ego tells them they deserve.

Navel-gazers are quickly seen by others as being on a never-ending emotional roller coaster. They experience lots of highs and lows that are not only expressed through anger and temper but also through depression, shirked responsibility, envy, gossip, insecurity, and isolation among other behaviors; the list goes on and on. Ruggeds, by contrast, develop the wisdom to know that volatile emotions are an incredible waste of time. They drain one of vital energy, disrupt teamwork, push people away, and ultimately, they have a detrimental effect on the entire organization. The only kind of roller coasters Ruggeds relish are the ones found in theme parks!

When the navel-gazers are in charge of a team, other members start playing it safe so as not to offend or make mistakes that draw the ire or retribution of that leader. Ruggeds have the wisdom to know that you need all of the people on a team playing to win. Playing it safe is counter to that mission. Because of this knowledge, Ruggeds learn to control their anger, use it sparingly, or redirect it. They often forgive mistakes they sense have been made in the spirit of trying new things because they want to maintain momentum and to encourage the team to keep innovating. When controlled properly, a Rugged uses their temper to focus, drive, inspire, and improve others' performances. Navel-gazers use it to elevate themselves, draw undue attention to themselves, and feed their ego. The benefits of controlling one's temper and making it a productive tool are monumental in business success. Its positive effect is amplified throughout the team and organization.

Navel-gazers don't associate wisdom with a mentality of abundance. Ruggeds DO!

The need to feed a gluttonous ego causes navel-gazers to hoard and keep secret the identities of expert sources they rely upon for help. They want the credit for all of the advice and support these experts offer to come their way. Their ego keeps them from understanding the abundance of information and wisdom that is available to them once they open their mind to it. They fail to learn that the more freely you recognize your lack of wisdom in relationship to the universe's abundance of it, the more open your consciousness becomes to that abundant wisdom. To come to this realization, one must be humble enough to see the connection. A lack of humility blocks the abundant thought process from occurring and keeps the navel-gazers zealously guarding the sources of new ideas as if no such thing as a library, the Internet, or people with more experience than them exists in the world.

Ruggeds learn that the world is big and the volume of wisdom it contains is not only plentiful, it is growing every day. They recognize that through humility they attract this wisdom. They understand that the key to opening Rugged Intellect lies in making the universe of wisdom come to them and they do this by being willing to give credit to the world of people, books, electronic media, nature, God, history, and so much more for sharing it with them. By humbly giving credit outwardly, the world becomes larger and more intimate at the same time. It seeks to bring you even more wisdom each time. This is especially true when your source of information is a person you have direct dealings with. When you freely access and give credit to others, they are apt to come back with even more useful information. They are also likely to acknowledge you for being fair. Then they'll tell others who may also be willing to share information with you. Giving credit where credit is due has a powerful multiplying affect that Ruggeds understand and appreciate precisely because they have Rugged Intellect.

**Navel-gazers don't easily form trusting relationships.
Ruggeds DO!**

Some of the navel-gazers I have studied tend to waste possibilities for meaningful relationships. This is a tragedy. They often have brilliant minds but have a difficult time developing and keeping trust. Because most navel-gazers see themselves as superior to others, envy and jealousy arise whenever they get close enough to really see the good in someone else. These resentments inhibit and destroy any prospect for lasting trust. Navel-gazers often engage in gossip and putting others down to raise themselves up. While all leaders have to assess and sometimes discuss people's strengths and weaknesses with others as part of evaluating their performance, Rugged leaders do so in a way that looks to avoid and prevent gossip. Their discussions focus on constructive ways to help lead or improve a person. It is never used as a way to boost oneself by putting others down. That behavior would quickly be perceived by others as nastiness contrived for intentional, self-serving purposes as opposed to being truthful for the advancement of good.

In the worst cases, some navel-gazers will go so far as to tell untruthful stories about others. As those working with navel-gazers start to hear their rumormongering and witness their deceptions, a cloud of distrust forms. With the addition of credit-hogging and blame-laying, it isn't long before the navel-gazer loses most, if not all, of the trust from others.

Ruggeds learn that trusting relationships are essential to the accomplishment of great feats. The cultivation of trusting interactions and partnerships is of the utmost importance. Through Rugged Intellect, entrepreneurs can grow ever wiser about how skilled communication creates confidence in collaborations. Study any Rugged and you will find a leader who has earned the kind of long-term, win-win business relationships that are mostly absent in a navel-gazer's experience. A Rugged's trustworthiness lets the world know volumes about his or her business persona and character. Think about how valuable that type of reputation is on the larger business landscape as well as within a Rugged's own organization. Given the reach of social media these days, this concept has an amplified effect.

Navel-gazers don't embrace a deep sense of personal responsibility. Ruggeds DO!

Because they aggressively seek credit, rarely believe they are wrong, avoid admitting mistakes, and often become emotional when confronted about even understandable errors, navel-gazers are not exactly known for having a deep sense of personal responsibility. The reverse of this behavior is what we all know and appreciate as accountability. Accountability creates the ownership mentality required for completing tasks, executing projects, and overseeing others well. Developing this quality makes Ruggeds exceptional business leaders. Such responsibility extends outward beyond those they oversee to include other individuals and team members throughout the organization. Everyone learns to shoulder the weight for mistakes made within the group.

When one is missing this quality, they become infected by what David Schwartz calls "excusitis"—a failure disease that he addresses in chapter two of his book, *The Magic of Thinking Big*. Ruggeds develop a NO EXCUSES mentality as part of their working persona. In part, it is Rugged Intellect that guides one to humbly embrace responsibility, ban excuses, eliminate blame, and thus become even more trusted by others for doing so. Great and highly productive teams thrive in this kind of atmosphere. When team members can count on getting credit for their contributions and not being blasted for the mistakes they make, they develop a love for being on that Rugged's team, and they look for any opportunity to join his or her efforts. How much more dynamic is it for a Rugged to attract that kind of allegiance when forming teams?

Ruggeds understand through their wisdom that by accepting more responsibility, more opportunity is given to them. The benefit of this is exponential. A Rugged's ability to be responsible for more enables him or her to continue to build higher and higher skyscrapers. Because Ruggeds are viewed by others as possessing this deep sense of personal responsibility, they are frequently asked to be on advisory boards and to be involved in a variety of impactful civic and business projects. Taking an owner's level of responsibility in just about everything they do inspires people's faith in them. When Ruggeds' reputations become publicly synonymous with this depth of personal responsibility, it is a great advertisement for the organizations they build.

Navel-gazers don't see failure as a necessary part of achieving success. Ruggeds DO!

When navel-gazers avoid accepting responsibility for mistakes, being wrong, or for things just not going well, they miss out on the power of failure teaching them necessary lessons. Ruggeds understand that a mistake or failure doesn't have to keep them from getting to their ultimate destination. They also know that it is not possible to avoid all mistakes. Ruggeds learn that mistakes and failures are a necessary part of improving oneself and one's business, and that *owning* failure empowers them to gain wisdom. When others see that you own your responsibility, they begin to take responsibility too. By far the most famous story of someone consistently seeing failure as a steppingstone to success is the one I'll recount for you next. It is almost hard to believe, but once you read it, you will recognize its truth and will commit it to your memory where I hope it will help you embrace your own failures.

Failing in business as a 22-year-old, he ran for state legislature at 23. After losing his state legislature race, he started another business at age 24. After failing in business again at age 25, he endured another blow—the love of his life died when he was just 26. All of this led to his having a nervous breakdown at the age of 27, which took years to recover from. After getting back on his feet at age 34, he ran for Congress, lost, and then ran again at age 39. Wouldn't you know it, he was defeated for a second time. At 46 he decided to run for Senate and lost, was selected to be on the ticket for vice president at 47. As was the trend, he found himself on the losing side of that election too. Accepting responsibility for all of his failures, he chose to run for Senate again at 49 and, you guessed it, he lost another time. Because he learned to embrace failure, own it, learn from it, and create wisdom around it, Abraham Lincoln decided he was ready for the office of president and ran one more time at the age of 51. He won the election and became president of the United States of America, occupying the highest office in the land. Because he had developed through each of his failures, he was ready to become one of the greatest presidents in our nation's history.

I strongly believe that by owning his failures and embracing the lessons that came from each of those experiences, President Lincoln learned how to persevere. I am convinced those failures and his humility paved the way for his great success as a leader through some of America's most challenging times. Failure appears to be a great teacher, wouldn't you agree?

One of the most famous college basketball coaches of all time, John Wooden, earned the nickname the Wizard of Westwood—Westwood, of course, referred to his team's home court. He got the nickname while winning ten NCAA Championships over a twelve-year stretch coaching men's basketball at UCLA. I consider the following quote from him a cure-all for anyone struggling with failure. Navel-gazers, in particular, might want to remember it for what it suggests will happen if you don't embrace failure. Coach Wooden profoundly said, *"Failure isn't fatal, but failure to change might be."*

Navel-gazers don't look to be Kingmakers. Ruggeds DO!

Navel-gazers bask in the limelight and love for the spotlight to be on them continuously. Ruggeds also love the spotlight. In fact, they likely love it even more than the navel-gazer. *Whoa, you may be thinking, doesn't that make Ruggeds navel-gazers too?* I know you navel-gazers reading this statement hope to see some hypocrisy in Rugged Intellect, but you won't find it here. Navel-gazers love the spotlight because they love the glory it gives them. Ruggeds love the spotlight because they see it as an opportunity to direct and shine that light on other people. Ruggeds understand that when they, their team, or their organization earns the spotlight, it is their responsibility to shift that spotlight towards others so as to lift them up and let them shine brightly in it. Ruggeds comprehend the wisdom behind building an organization of kings. The thought and responsibility of becoming kingmakers genuinely excite them. Navel-gazers, on the other hand, rarely *share* the spotlight, let alone cast it on someone else and possibly elevate them to an equal or higher status—especially someone who reports directly to them. Navel-gazers fear losing the talent beneath them because using those people is how they manipulated the spotlight to shine on themselves in the first place. The last thing they want is for someone to whisk that talent away. The navel-gazer's nature is the antithesis of the kingmaker's. It keeps others hidden.

Navel-gazers hoard talent yet they don't invest in the talent's development for fear of deflecting credit away from themselves. What they don't realize is how much more talent and wisdom can be unleashed when you commit to developing your teams. Because Ruggeds believe in abundance, they are not afraid of cultivating talent or of losing it either. When people are treated well, when the spotlight is shined on them, too, and when they rise to new heights as a result, a deep sense of loyalty is fostered and attrition remains low. Even if talent leaves for new opportunities, Ruggeds are confident they can continuously attract and develop new talent to their teams and organizations. Ruggeds truly understand the wisdom in elevating others, even above themselves, if doing so empowers the team or organization to achieve greater success. Ruggeds embrace the wisdom of reciprocity and know well that reciprocity isn't just about giving and receiving benefit; it's about *multiplying* benefit for everyone. Ruggeds have also learned the cyclical nature of the spotlight: the more they shine it on others, the more the world turns the spotlight back on them and they are able to go another round of shining that light on even more talent. Once a Rugged starts to become known as a kingmaker, talent is automatically easier for them to attract. Kingmakers are vital to Rugged organizations for their incredibly strong team-building abilities.

Navel-gazers don't generally value and seek out critical advice. Ruggeds DO!

If you want to measure the success and experience level of a Rugged Entrepreneur, one of the best tells is to look at how good their personal and organizational coaches and advisors are. The more successful and experienced a Rugged's group of personal and organizational coaches and advisors happens to be, the more successful that Rugged is likely to already be. Just as iron sharpens iron, so does one Rugged sharpen another. Navel-gazers have too much unhealthy pride to ask other accomplished people to be their personal coach and advisor. In the rare cases when they do ask or gain access to a coach or advisor, the process of opening themselves up to the critique that is necessary for growth and change is generally too frustrating for them. Because their ego cannot accept the advice being offered warmly, navel-gazers tend to spend too much of their time in these sessions debating and exhausting the coach's energy and patience.

As Ruggeds grow their organization(s), so grows their need to access a greater level of wisdom. Thus, a team of business and personal advisors and coaches are invaluable. If you are looking to become a Rugged or are in the early stages of being one, I suggest that you seek the counsel of the most successful entrepreneurs you can gain access to and ask them to give you some time as an advisor or coach. Then respect them and yourself by opening up to their constructive evaluation and criticism. And definitely be appreciative of their time and willingness to offer their advice. My personal and business advisors all know they have carte blanche to tell me I am being stupid anytime they see fit. I don't always agree with all of my advisors' advice, but I always listen to and ponder what they have to say. I often apply some or all of it to my life or businesses accordingly.

When I first formed Retail Service Systems, I asked Jerry Williams, who was already well known in the home furnishings world, to intro-duce me to the person whom he felt was the most connected to the then 95-billion-dollar-a-year U.S. home furnishings industry. Within a few days, Jerry told me that he had arranged an introduction to that very man, Bob O'Neill. I was to meet him at my first furniture market coming up in a few weeks. Bob was a man with forty-plus years of high-level furniture industry experience; he had started in sales, then built and sold a multi-million-dollar company, run an entire division of a billion-dollar-plus organization, and sat on numerous boards including the initial World Market Board, which houses the Vegas furniture market twice a year.

When Jerry ultimately made the introduction, I quickly told Bob that I had strong experience in business and distribution but knew very little about the home furnishings industry. I then proceeded to tell him how Jerry viewed him as the most experienced person he knew in the business and I literally asked him, "Will you give me some time and take me under your wing? I'd appreciate some critical advice and coaching." Thank God he said, "Certainly." Lessons I have learned from numerous conversations with Bob resonate in several sections of this book.

During one of those advisory conversations with Bob, I was boasting about how large one of our companies could get without hitting the 50-employee threshold. When a company has more than fifty employees, they are mandated to provide a health plan for all. Now, I am not against having health plans for our employees and had already been an owner of other businesses that provided them. I was just against the nightmare mess it poses and the irresponsible navel-gazing politicians who created the laws to try to regulate the industry from afar. I was hopeful that the flawed system would get resolved through deregulation so free enterprise capitalism could have a better chance to go to work in that space.

Over dinner one evening I explained to Bob that I felt it would be several years before the government actually fixed health care in a way that was conducive for a small business owner to offer a great plan, and that I'd rather just pay people enough to get a health plan on their own. I told him that under that premise, my goal was to grow the company to have fewer than fifty employees to avoid triggering the government-enforced healthcare. Bob instantly said, "You're being stupid. If you really thought big, you would be trying to think, *What does the company need to do in order to grow successfully to five hundred employees as fast as it can, and not have to care about the governmental health care mess?*"

A great advisor is one who widens your scope, giving you the ability to see things better. If you are not open to his or her critique, then having an advisor is irrelevant. Bob remains one of my treasured life and business advisors to this day. Do you have access to any highly successful people who would be willing to empower you by giving you critical advice? Accepting even tough advice from a coach is a lot easier than receiving it from someone who directly reports to you, so let's look at one last story for an example of what can happen when peers or those who report to you offer criticism. (Something a navel-gazer would despise!)

The same year that one of the companies I founded ranked in the top 20 percent of *Inc.* magazine's 5000 Fastest Growing Companies list for a *second* time, some of the other companies we owned were also experiencing comfortable success. Given these successes and the need to move forward with writing *The Rugged Entrepreneur,* among other related commitments, I had purposely begun to back out of the spotlight in parts of that organization. In my mind, I had made enough Kings there to move into its shadows. I had comfortably gained thirty pounds and was looking forward to slowing down and becoming somewhat of a recluse with my wife, who is my best friend. I liked working from home, going days without shaving, and even prided myself on avoiding social media completely. Then one day, a key team member who reported directly to me critically reminded me that it was my responsibility to be the public face of the company in its second wave of publicity. He also said that if I didn't create a public persona through social media, get in good shape, and consider doing infomercials on Rugged Entrepreneurialism to magnify that brand, I would be hurting our company's growth capabilities and thus, hurting its people.

His and other teammates' criticisms on the subject were warranted, and while it was the kind of tough cut that would have angered a navel-gazer, I knew that as a Rugged, I had to take those words to heart. Because I've learned the value and strength of embracing humility, had respect for this person's wisdom, and had developed a deep sense of personal responsibility, I set up the right social media platforms for myself to help represent our company well. Upon looking in the mirror, I realized that I did need to improve my physical health. Any image to the contrary would not be beneficial to our business, especially when we were in the spotlight. So I lost 30 pounds and made sure I stayed clean-shaven whenever I was in public. That critical advice, my willingness to heed it, and my ability to take action prompted me to complete this very book.

Hearing and accepting critical advice aren't comfortable, and it's certainly not for the mentally weak. That's why it's included here as a

Rugged trait. Ruggeds surround themselves with critical advisors and then consider their advice with an open mind. You do not have to agree with all of what is said, nor do you have to do everything the way the person offering that advice thinks you should, but you do have to be willing to look at things through their lenses with an intent to improve yourself and your organization(s).

Navel-gazers do not find comfort in apologizing. Ruggeds DO!

Being apologetic is an aspect of being humble. It is also an aspect of building and maintaining trusting relationships and embracing failure. When an apology begins with "If," it is likely coming from a navel-gazer. "If I offended you, then I am sorry." "If what I did messed you up, then I am sorry." Beginning with the big "If" is often the way the navel-gazer deflects half or more of the blame on the very person to whom they should be apologizing. It means that maybe an apology shouldn't even be made. The apology is less than sincere.

Also, do not misunderstand this about apologizing: In today's dangerously politically correct climate where a bunch of non-Rugged cream puffs claim to be offended by any and all criticism, one can end up being too apologetic. Apologizing must be real and for something that warrants an apology. As you already know, being a Rugged, and building up people, teams, and organizations, requires making and embracing mistakes. Often those mistakes come in the form of missing a meeting or being late for a meeting (something you should try never to do, though it sometimes happens due to unforeseen circumstances). When others have given their valuable time to prepare and be present at an appointed time, a Rugged who delays a meeting or who cannot make it is truly sorry and sincerely apologizes.

Sometimes our emotions get the best of us or we miscommunicate in a way that is condescending or angered. Our Rugged Intellect tells us when this is happening, and our humility is such that we can sincerely apologize for the offense so as to protect the relationship and trust we've already established between us. Navel-gazers lack the intellect or the desire to make things right in such instances. Because of that, they actually experience discomfort at the thought of apologizing and rarely say they are sorry for anything they do. As a result, the navel-gazer has a much more difficult time retaining great people or building open and fully productive relationships with them.

Ruggeds work hard to bring the visions they have for their companies to fruition, but as is the case for anyone who casts a dream and runs to chase it, they may fall short on some of their goals. In falling short, an organization's owner can easily find people or circumstances to point fingers at. They can blame supply chain problems, legal problems, personnel problems, or a host of other problems for the mistake. The blame list for someone with "excusitis" is endless. By contrast, a Rugged Intellect teaches us to pull our own thumb long before we point an accusatory finger at someone else.

When Ruggeds make mistakes, they set out to analyze and correct them. They begin by tapping into universal wisdom and asking what they could have done differently or better to avoid this mistake. Then they use the answers to make sincere apologies to the people, team, and organization affected, or possibly even to the public. These apologies typically come with a pledge or plan for moving forward. In doing this, Ruggeds endear themselves to others. By being properly apologetic, they have set an example of humility and self-reflection and have evidenced that the well-being of the whole is more important to them than their ego. A sincere and thoughtful apology helps them build great teams. However, when someone apologizes too much, or in a manner that is insincere, they end up being perceived as fake. Ruggeds are not fake.

Being humble is the key to opening the mind and heart wide enough to build a Rugged Intellect. It enables one to seek, accept, and grow in knowledge.

The universe of shared wisdom that is infinite in quantity and connected to everything is something many describe as spiritual in nature. It is also very practical and effective.

Alter Egos

While this discussion has placed a lot of emphasis on humility, please do not think that Ruggeds give more weight to this trait than they do to pride. Rugged Entrepreneurs consider healthy pride to be as important a characteristic as humility. Humility is only discussed first because without it, the doorway to a Rugged Intellect remains closed. An egocentric person who has read this far, but who doesn't wish to embrace humility can still rise to an incredibly high level and succeed as an entrepreneur, but their experiences will be quite different from a complete Rugged Entrepreneur.

Throughout my lifetime of studying capitalism, free enterprise, and entrepreneurialism, and certainly throughout my time becoming a Rugged Entrepreneur, I have identified three specific types of entrepreneurs: Rugged Entrepreneurs, Professional Entrepreneurs, and Corporate Entrepreneurs. Some of the best and most successful Professional and Corporate Entrepreneurs I know can be extremely egocentric. In many ways their work demands it. They are proof that you can have a very present and large ego and still be a huge success as an entrepreneur. Maybe one of these other types of entrepreneurialism is better suited for you as you strive to be the best entrepreneur you can be.

A Professional Entrepreneur, as I define it, is a business owner in a highly skilled and often licensed field. Examples include doctors, lawyers, consultants, architects, builders, accountants, financiers, real estate brokers, and so forth. The work of many of these Professional Entrepreneurs is done independently. Their business is largely conducted on a one-on-one basis with a client and is often less about building large organizational teams. Professional Entrepreneurs are frequently, though not always, better equipped for their work when they have exuberant egos. They must convey and believe in their capabilities above all others' abilities in order to handle what's at stake for their clients, which can often be their life, livelihood, freedom, safety, or savings. Of course, not all surgeons have to be egoists to perform surgery, though it can be a very helpful and empowering trait to have when operating on someone's heart or brain, for instance. Similarly, not all attorneys are egoists, though it may be a quality you want them to possess when they are arguing a position with an opponent that could either cost, save, or make you millions. Simply put, an egocentric person is more apt to win those kinds of challenges when everyone around them believes they are one of the best at doing what they do.

Corporate Entrepreneurs, as I define them, have a large enough ego to want to forgo having a boss, but they do not have the interest in or necessarily want to go through the educational or licensing process to become a Professional Entrepreneur. A Corporate Entrepreneur is generally an individual who desires to work in a structured environment with relatively established practices and still have the freedom to be in business for themselves. Franchise businesses tend to provide the ideal balance of structure and independence for them. In a pure franchise enterprise, a franchisor creates and refines a business model that can be duplicated successfully in other locations. The franchisor then licenses these rights to an individual owner/operator to own and run the business. The owner/operators are called "franchisees." Although the franchisors maintain control of the overarching franchise, franchisees enjoy the combination of structure and independence this set-up affords. Their ego needs are met because they are the bosses of their own domain, but their risk and the time demanded of them to perfect the business is minimized since the business model has already been tried and tested by the franchisor. Corporate Entrepreneurs who become franchisees are essentially given the tools to launch their business in a structured environment. Then it is up to them to apply the model successfully.

You do not have to be a Rugged to succeed in businesses like these; however, all of the lessons about being a Rugged Entrepreneur that I share in this book can certainly help you as a Professional or Corporate Entrepreneur.

Rugged Entrepreneurs can be found in almost any kind of business. From the start, Ruggeds learn to have and develop a strong and healthy pride as opposed to an ego.

They learn why such pride is important and how to wield it properly because their success is contingent on building people, teams, and organizations that also develop, grow, and share a healthy pride. Rugged Pride is not hubristic. Wherever it applies to a Professional or Corporate Entrepreneur's business, they should add a measure of healthy pride if they do not already. It is taking delight in one's accomplishments, finding gratification in working hard, solving problems creatively, accepting personal responsibility, sacrificing, being loyal, acknowledging others, and upholding the ideals of honesty, purpose, passion, leadership, and commitment to mission. Rugged Pride also directs energy towards identifying, developing, and edifying those same qualities in others.

When a Rugged's pride shows, it is a reflection on the work of the entire team. Seeing a Rugged's outward pride directed at the accomplishments of others creates camaraderie and an extended organizational pride that is one of the secrets to a company's success. It goes a long way toward building forward momentum and a strong corporate culture. A healthy pride inspires others to emulate the same qualities exhibited by the Rugged Entrepreneur leader. Healthy pride reduces turnover and fosters a team sense of ownership over the mission of the organization. When one has a healthy pride, they rarely make comparisons to other team members or to outside organizations because a Rugged's wisdom tells them that there will always be *betters* or *lessers* down the road.

Comparing oneself, others, or the organization as a whole to anyone else only leads to envy or arrogance, and neither is productive or healthy.

I love the poem "Desiderata" by Max Ehrmann. The word "desiderata" in Latin means "things desired," and the poem is about having desirable qualities in life. I encountered it in college and one of the primary life lessons I learned about having the right balance of humility and pride came from the line in that poem that I used as the epigraph for this chapter, *"If you compare yourself with others, you may become vain and bitter; for always there will be greater and lesser persons than yourself."* Finding and committing such wisdom to memory can help you maintain just the right proportion of humility and pride that I talk about as *healthy Rugged Pride.*

The great basketball coach John Wooden, whom I referenced earlier, understood and avoided the trappings of comparisons. He was not only known for his many championship wins, he was also known for running his teams' offense and game plan without ever focusing on the other teams' defense. He believed that if UCLA executed its offense as well as its players could, and if they played strong defense, they didn't have to focus on their opponents' team members or strategy. Essentially, he believed in making your offense so good that the competition has to worry about you and not the other way around. This is a great example of healthy pride.

In the organizations our teams build, we know about the industry and about competitors, but we take pride in our mission of obsessively focusing on our customers so that our business offense is good enough to not have to continuously compare what we do to what others are doing. When you have that kind of pride, it is noticed by your people and duplicated. I love organizations with this kind of pride because they almost always set the pace and standard for excellence for the rest of their industry or market.

As we discussed, Ruggeds should first have pride in others. But when it applies directly to themselves, a Rugged's pride needs to be based, at least in part, on sacrifice. "Sacrifice" is another word that creates an emotional word-picture memory for me. The definition is one that stretches back to a more ancient time when most people raised livestock and offered the best of their herd or flock in sacrifice to God. Imagine burning an animal as an offering after putting so much time, resources, and energy into raising it. This is a harsh image, but one that a person isn't likely to forget.

A Rugged knows the sacrifice he or she has made and doesn't wear it on their shirtsleeve. Instead, they hold it in their mind and heart where it helps them make good decisions. The personal sacrifice of finances, time, sweat, and wisdom are important aspects of a Rugged's inner pride. It is also how a Rugged comes to appreciate the people he or she works with. Because Ruggeds have had to sacrifice, they clearly recognize, understand, and value the sacrifice of others. Of course, you don't have to experience something yourself in order to see it in someone else, but having that deep mutual understanding gives Ruggeds a greater appreciation for that sacrifice when they witness it. By contrast, people who have not sacrificed much, or at all, rarely notice or appreciate such gestures.

One of several inspiring pictures I have in my office is of a work called *Praying Hands* by Albrecht Dürer. It is an image of great fame, hung on walls in many homes around the world. The original pen-and-ink drawing is over four-hundred years old and while the truth of the lore surrounding it has long been debated, the prevailing story makes a lasting emotional and visual association with the word "sacrifice" even more powerful than the one of sacrificing a prized animal.

The short version of the story goes something like this: Having come from a poor family of eighteen children, Albrecht and one of his brothers drew straws to determine which of them would go to work blacksmithing in the mines to pay for the other to go to art school in Nuremburg. According to their deal, the first who went to school would come home upon graduation and teach, sell art, or work in some other way to support the second brother's training at school in Nuremburg.

Albrecht won the draw, so his brother soon went to work blacksmithing in the mines where he earned the money to pay for Albrecht's education. As promised, Albrecht returned home four years later and told his brother it was now time for him to become an artist. With tears in his eyes, the brother held up his hands, which had been injured and bruised from his toils in the mines. "Brother," he said to Albrecht, "my hands have been broken and calloused so as to be rendered incapable of even holding a brush steady enough to paint a fair stroke. I can no longer be the artist so you will have to paint for me."

It's often been said that the inspiration for the world-famous *Praying Hands* and the rest of Albrecht's art was the great sacrifice his brother made for him—the sacrifice of his own hands. I have a print of that painting in my office to remind me that you must make sacrifices, that it's okay to be proud of them, and that it is important to acknowledge and honor the sacrifices of others. That picture hangs near a statue of a soldier kneeling at a tombstone with this inscription:

> *"Greater love hath no man than this, that a*
> *man lay down his life for his friends."*
> —John 15:13

In all three of my offices, I have similar reminders of sacrifice and how mine has always been outmatched by the many others who came before me. These emotional images help me maintain the balance between humility and the Rugged Pride we've been talking about. They serve as a guiding compass for me.

My most-endearing memory associated with sacrifice is that of me taking my grandfather back to Normandy, France, when he was eighty-five years old. The last time he had been to Normandy was sixty-five years earlier. At the youthful age of twenty, he parachuted into the region with thermite grenades strapped to his legs on a mission to blow up German anti-aircraft guns. My grandfather, like so many other 18- to 21-year-old young men, volunteered to fight overseas and help liberate others in WWII. He told me that in training, he signed up to be a para-trooper for the extra fifteen dollars danger-pay per month. Parachutes for cargo had been around for over 100 years but using paratroopers as a force was an entirely new concept. Passenger airplanes large enough to carry them had only recently been designed, and WWII was the first time a para-dropping strategy was being employed in war. All of the other D-Day pilots and paratroopers were largely as young and inex-perienced as my grandfather. Many had never flown in combat. But the Germans, who had fortified Normandy with heavy anti-aircraft artillery and machine guns, were very prepared for the D-Day landing. Their defense was so formidable that their firepower and anti-aircraft flack sent American planes scattering everywhere. Almost none of the paratroopers was dropped in their targeted drop zones. As gliders and planes crashed, many men were killed, including Brigadier General Don Forrester Pratt, the highest-ranking officer to perish on D-Day.

In the chaos, hundreds of American paratroopers such as my grand-father landed miles away from where they were supposed to. To their credit and bravery, they improvised, banding together in small gueril-la-type groups of four to ten men moving across the land in an attempt to engage the enemy and fulfill their mission. What could have easily been a failure, ultimately turned into success, as the broad spread of troops moving in all directions confused the Germans into thinking the invading force was everywhere and many times larger than it really was. As American soldiers confronted enemy troops in multiple locations, the panicking Germans could be heard unraveling in subsequent radio transmissions. As it happened, that panic became a strategic advantage for the Allies.

I took my grandfather back to Normandy with the intent of finding his targets—the original anti-aircraft gun placements he was charged with taking out—and to find the farmhouse where he and some other intrepid soldiers liberated a French family who were being forced to live in their barn. We connected with another veteran paratrooper from the 101st Airborne, and I was able to engage an off-duty French Army Captain, who lived in the area and was familiar with the history, to help us find the places we were looking for. It took us two days, but we finally saw what we came to see. My grandfather has since passed away, but I will never forget us finding that farm and seeing him kiss the cheek of the eighty-one-year-old woman still living there, just as she had been at age sixteen when my grandfather and some other young Americans liberated her and her family. It is a memory that is etched into my mind and was the only time I ever saw my grandfather cry.

On the same bookshelf in my office that holds the statue of the kneeling soldier I mentioned earlier, there are many other items honoring our great military troops. There you will find, among other treasures, my grandfather's coffin flag, some photos of him, his medals, and a newspaper article about our trip. It is humbling to think about the sacrifices American soldiers like my grandfather made, not just to protect America but to liberate others from tyranny. If you ever travel to Normandy and see the cemeteries where thousands of young Americans who gave their lives are buried, it will move you to tears. It has left an indelible impression of sacrifice in my mind and heart. Ruggeds respect and appreciate sacrifice and treasure those who were and still are willing to make it.

Again, it's important to remember that while Rugged Pride is healthy, we are all imperfect beings and will sometimes allow our pride to get the best of us, or even influence us to make some poor decisions. Those decisive actions influenced by pride will get you into a little bit of trouble at times and may even get you into *a lot* of trouble if you're not careful. One way to help you minimize the number of incidences is to identify an emotional story where your own pride, or someone else's in relationship to you, created a deep memory you just cannot forget. Mark the story in your head as an example of what to think about whenever you see unhealthy pride being a problem for someone around you. It's not something to use as a corrective measure with them; rather, it is a personal reminder to condition yourself not to fall prey to pride's trap. Daphene and I recall this emotional picture with one word: horses.

Having owned horses and a rodeo production company, I grew accustomed to people around me discussing these animals as if they understood them merely because they had rented and ridden a stable horse a few times in their life. On those rides, they certainly learned some basic skills in maneuvering a trained horse, but they came nowhere close to attaining the kind of wisdom one acquires from raising and dealing with spirited horses. One of mine was a 16-hand Thoroughbred named Killian, and, boy, did that horse love to run.

People who are not trained to handle a horse like that generally try a gentle or polite tact, but common sense should tell them that if just being polite could get an extremely powerful animal to completely cooperate, horses wouldn't need steel bits in their mouths.

If Killian was out and wanted to run but his rider expected him to go back to the stable, the horse would turn mean and often dash anyway. Several times, friends who came with me to the stables would say, "I'd love to ride Killian. Can I?" My response was always, "He's a great horse, but do you really know how to ride and handle an animal with some spirit?" Most of them, being a little too prideful, would say, "Sure, I've been riding since I was a teenager" or something to that effect when in actuality, all they had done was some stable riding at summer camp a few times. These weren't navel-gazers, but in this situation they were clueless. Sure enough, if I let them, they would casually ride this specimen of a horse past the barn and into the field just beyond the coral, where Killian then thought it was time to run. The closer he got to that point, the more the rider could feel Kilian's desire to roam free. All of a sudden, sitting on top of that very tall and very powerful animal, they'd get a little scared of his power and quickly try to bring him back around towards the corral. In that moment, Killian would sometimes let loose with a rear or a kick before bursting full force into a run. If the rider tried to rein him back and bring him around, Killian was likely to try and sideswipe him into a tree. The mental picture of one of my very tough, mountain raised, redneck friends (who shall remain nameless here to protect his bruised ego) screaming and diving off a speeding horse before he would have likely been rammed into a tree, makes me laugh inside every time (I'm doing so as I write this).

That's the emotional word-picture story that comes to mind every time I need to remember just how much trouble a person can get into when their ego answers for them. Daff and I give each other a knowing look and just have to say the code word "horses" to each other when we're dealing with someone whose ego is getting in the way of being real, and thus, of them being their best in a team effort. Once again, I tell you, using emotional word-picture stories is a great way to create a perpetual reminder of lessons you've already learned. You can use them with or without having to point them out externally. Such lessons help you keep your own pride and humility in balance. What story do you have about yourself or someone else that can serve as your "horses" memory?

Further Points of Pride

In today's world of twenty-four-hour-a-day, seven-day-a-week access to the Internet and social media, companies should absolutely learn how to use their online presence(s) in ways that instill and promote a healthy pride about what their organization does and who its people are. In one of our licensing and franchising companies, BoxDrop™ Mattress & Furniture, we have a CCO (Chief Community Officer) named Darren Conrad. Darren is a great Rugged and a guru in the mattress retailing industry. We consider his incredible talent for connecting with people, both personally and through social media, as extremely important— possibly even more important to our organization than his business genius and training capabilities. Darren recognizes how vital connectivity is and how it helps build organizational pride the right way. His awareness of this dynamic, and his skill for implementing it throughout a large organization, earned him an equity position in RSS that he treasures and is very proud of. I will talk more about the importance of the CCO role in an organization, and specifically about connectivity, in a subsequent section on community as a Rugged skill, but I mention it here as it is indeed an important part of building healthy organizational pride.

I find it shocking how few companies and their leaders truly understand organizational pride and its merits. Sometimes the company leadership is misguided in its goals. I see this frequently in many of the private equity-owned companies that have permeated America's business landscape. Often their goals are so tied to short-term financial measurements that the leaders don't set building organizational pride as an objective. Sometimes these private equity "gunslingers" are egocentric to the point of being navel-gazers. It may be that their exuberant confidence is good for the short-term business plan, driven less by relationships than by revenues and margins, but it's not good for building pride in an organization. Even if it's decided that the best plan for a business is focusing on short-term goals (an approach I would argue against), there are still ways a leader can have and demonstrate organizational pride, and its importance to individual and corporate growth.

CHAPTER FOUR

FORTITUDO MENTIS (AKA, MENTAL TOUGHNESS)

"We've won a lot of different ways under a lot of different circumstances. This mental toughness, man, that's what it's all about, and this team's got it."
—Tom Brady, Patriots Four-Time Super Bowl Champion
Quarterback on their miraculous comeback win
against the Atlanta Falcons in Super Bowl LI

THE WORDS *FORTITUDO MENTIS* HAVE A POWERFUL AND VICTORIOUS ring to them. Writing them out and placing them somewhere you are sure to see frequently is a great way to remind yourself of the concept we call "mental toughness." These words just seem to echo the ancient ethos of warrior leaders who were as strong in mind as they were strong in battle. Perhaps this history is what makes the Latin phrase resonate so strongly with today's leaders.

Mental toughness is a complex character trait whose components have been observed, studied, and written about for thousands of years. Chinese, Icelandic, Greek, Egyptian, Roman, Japanese, Indian, and literally every other ancient culture all developed proverbs and lore surrounding the components of mental toughness. These recorded life lessons for success in their cultures included maintaining willpower, handling objections, facing truth, persevering, focusing, overcoming fear with action, being resilient, and having grit among many other attributes of the mind.

Mental toughness has become such a popular and broadly taught concept in educational coaching and mentorship programs that it can be seen executed in sports, the military, and certainly in the business world among entrepreneurs and corporate leaders. Because so many accomplished people have been quoted acknowledging the power of mental toughness, a fun way to learn from them is to read as many of those quotes as possible. Here are a few of my favorites:

"Mental toughness is many things and rather difficult to explain. Its qualities are sacrifice and self-denial. It is humility because it behooves all of us to remember that simplicity is the sign of greatness and meekness is the sign of true strength. Mental Toughness is Spartanism with qualities of sacrifice, self-denial, dedication, fearlessness, and love."
—Vince Lombardi

"Nothing can stop the man with the right mental attitude from achieving his goal; nothing on earth can help the man with the wrong mental attitude."
—Thomas Jefferson

*"The most important attribute a player
must have is mental toughness."*
—MIA HAMM

*"It takes energy, mental toughness and spiritual rein-
forcement to successfully deal with life's opportunities, and to reach your objectives."*
—ZIG ZIGLAR

*"It's when the discomfort strikes that they realize a
strong mind is the most powerful weapon of all."*
—CHRISSIE WELLINGTON

*"In training everyone focuses on 90 percent physical and 10
percent mental, but in the races it's 90 percent mental because
there's very little that separates us physically at the elite level."*
—ELKA GRAHAM

"Mental toughness is to physical as four is to one."
—BOBBY KNIGHT

*"Mental Toughness is the ability to consistently perform
toward the upper range of your talent and skill
regardless of the competitive circumstances."*
—JAMES E LOEHR

*"Strong minds suffer without complaining; weak
minds complain without suffering."*
—Lettie Cowman

*"Concentration and mental toughness
are the margins of victory."*
—Bill Russell

*"You have power over your mind, not outside events.
Realize this, and you will find strength."*
—Marcus Aurelius

*"A big thing in developing mental toughness is you want
people around you to tell you the truth in a moment. And
then are you willing to accept that truth in that moment? Or
do you find an excuse or do you rationalize? What do you
do? Or do you say, 'I got it. I got it.' The quicker that you
can get it, and the quicker that you can develop relationships with people that will tell you the truth, the better."*
—Mike Krzyzewski

*"Most Rugged Entrepreneurs have at least one stretch where they
have less money coming in than they have going out. Those Ruggeds
learn business survival on an <u>eat-what-you-kill basis</u>. Successfully
growing a business while having to eat what you kill and telling
no-one about the struggle, makes for one mentally tough Rugged."*
—Scott Andrew

Mental toughness has not only been explored by athletes, the military, and countless business leaders, it has been explored on a deep scientific level as well. I learned my favorite scientific definition of mental toughness reading a study entitled, "The Concept of Mental Toughness: Tests of Dimensionality, Nomological Network and Traitness," by Daniel F. Gucciardi, Sheldon Hanton, Sandy Gordon, Clifford J. Mallett, and Philip Temby. The study summarized its meaning as follows: *"Mental toughness is the presence of some or the entire collection of experientially developed and inherent values, attitudes, emotions, cognitions, and behaviors that influence the way in which an individual approaches, responds to, and appraises both negatively and positively construed pressures, challenges, and adversities to consistently achieve his or her goals."*

The word "experientially" is key in this statement, and for me it refers to my father always saying, *"If you're going to be stupid, you had better be tough."* My father's words reflect the fact that most of us learn mental toughness over time as we live life and make mistakes. But a Rugged doesn't just develop this quality by learning from the pain of past errors. They train themselves to look ahead, not just to look in a rear-view mirror. They set out to intentionally increase their mental toughness as a way to build a stronger foundation for themselves, their teams, and organizations. They develop it on purpose in everything they do so they can avert or overcome challenges, mistakes, and failures whenever they arise.

Let's break the scientific definition into sections to better understand it. We'll start at the end where the reason why mental toughness is such an important quality is stated. The definition explains that mental toughness is a measurable quality that an individual uses to *approach, respond to, and appraise negative and positive pressures, challenges, and adversities that he or she will face in their effort to succeed.* When you really narrow it down that way, it is easy to see why Rugged Entrepreneurs prioritize it and build it into the foundation of their life and business. The first half of the definition actually provides a blueprint to the source of mental toughness—it is in our *values, attitudes, cognitions, and behaviors, which collectively influence or determine the way we make decisions and act* in certain situations.

At this very moment, you have a certain level of mental toughness based on the experiences, failures, successes, skills, values, and intellect that you have already acquired in life. In the scientific definition, those are described as your "experiential collection." The great thing about learning this now is that you can take charge of developing your mental toughness from this point forward. How well you choose to protect and grow this essential element is completely up to you. It is a choice similar to the ones you've made if you've ever decided to diet or get into better physical shape. Any number of things can improve or weaken your mental toughness. What this all means is that you have a mental toughness quotient (MTQ); it is yours to increase or decrease according to your effort.

To improve your MTQ you can create a specific reading program, engage in a competitive sport, learn a complex game such as bridge, and develop associations with others who are positive, challenging, and mentally tough too. You can also spend time tapping into universal wisdom or meditating, particularly on issues pertaining to your business. Accepting responsibility for and tackling projects where something has to be built or improved is another great way to increase your MTQ.

Likewise, you should also be aware of habits, behaviors, and circumstances that weaken your mental toughness including doing drugs, abusing alcohol, being reckless with your health to the point that you are continuously tired, associating with extremely negative influencers, engaging in nothing but cognition-deficient entertainment, and failing to learn new skills or grow your mind through study. These are all things that can decrease your mental toughness quotient.

Long before I fully understood the concept of being a Rugged, I knew that mental toughness was an important aspect and skill for any entrepreneur to have. Because I owned several businesses, I was often asked to speak about what it takes to succeed. My favorite topic was mental toughness. I added the "quotient" element later to emphasize the magnitude and potential growth of this characteristic. To intentionally work on and increase my own mental toughness in a measurable way, I created a personal program using the acrostic R.A.I.S.E.M.E., which stands for: **R**eading, **A**ssociating, **I**nvesting, **S**urrounding, **E**ntertaining, **M**editating, and **E**ducating. Each letter is an action word because it takes action to increase your mental toughness quotient. Some of you who have heard me speak about this or who have known me for a long time may remember a time when the acrostic was R.A.I.S.E.M.T. with the "T" representing "Teach," but after sharing it with a very wise communicator by the name of Hope Innelli, she suggested that I make it R.A.I.S.E.M.E with the final "E" representing "Educate." She saw that it was easier to remember and it also works because raising your mental toughness is essential to raising yourself. My wife and I both embrace this acrostic, and it has become a personal program for how we both work on our mental toughness quotient together. Let me break it down a little more for you here:

"R" Is for Reading: Reading is a critical component to increasing mental toughness quickly. It is also a phenomenal way to improve one's wisdom in a very specific subject so you can become an expert in that area. Two factors make reading one of the most important actions to take when improving mental toughness.

First, reading is the only way I know to access lessons a proven expert spent years or even decades learning in just the time it takes to finish a single book. I am always amazed by how few people take advantage of another person's diligent labor in order to study this way. It is not as instantaneous as plugging into someone's head and downloading master-level jujitsu training as happens in movies such as *The Matrix*, but it is the closest thing there is to that.

I remember when I bought the book *Business at the Speed of Thought* by Bill Gates in early 1999. Gates had founded Microsoft in the spring of 1975 at the age of twenty and had become the world's wealthiest man just twenty years later in 1995. He topped that list for many years until Jeff Bezos surpassed him in 2018. At the time I picked up that book, the world was in the midst of an Internet boom, and I was trying to build a small business-to-business Internet-based distribution company. Lo and behold, a twenty-five-dollar book by a technology visionary willing to share what he knew about and believed would happen in that businesses is suddenly on sale at a bookstore near me! It was literally the best way to learn about using and adapting to the new technology that was available. It's a thick book—almost five hundred pages long—with an immense amount of information on what Gates saw happening at the time and also what he predicted for the future of business in the digital electronic age.

I took the book to the gym every day after leaving my office and read it with a highlighter and pen in hand while working out on the tread climber—a machine that's ideal for getting a good cardio workout while reading at the same time. I rarely saw anyone else even skim a book while exercising, but there I was gaining the best of what a technology genius and multibillionaire could teach me about how innovations in that field would impact business in general, and my business more specifically. Years' worth of his wisdom were all in one book and it only cost me about twenty-five bucks and the effort to dive right in. It took me two and a half weeks to get through it from the beginning to the end. But how long do you think it took Bill Gates to acquire all of that wisdom and vision?

That book—from someone who had forgotten more than I would ever know about technology—helped me gain insight, develop ideas, and ultimately build a successful Internet business. Reading it not only added to my knowledge, but it made me feel more confident and mentally tough. How could I *not* feel that way? The experience was like getting a personal coaching session from Bill Gates himself. I was accessing his wisdom as if we were some type of business partners (in my mind of course!), while most of my competitors were not. Knowing that most people don't have a reading regime, but I do, gave me a competitive advantage. It was something I could control and train myself to enjoy and be proud of. Reading gives you an edge that most others don't have or even seek to have. It gives you a mental toughness—true cognitive strength over your competitors. It also relates back to the whole topic of deservance, as discussed earlier. Because a Rugged feels worthy of receiving knowledge, he or she pursues it, usually from the most reliable and accomplished sources.

No matter what topic you wish to improve upon or learn about, there are volumes of books written by incredible experts, teachers, coaches, millionaires, billionaires, spiritual leaders, politicians, military commanders, corporate executives, entrepreneurs, professional athletes, historians, and many other people who have overcome great obstacles to know what they do—people who have built wonders, and people who have studied others. The knowledge you then add to your own is something you will also share in conversations and corporate communications of all kinds. When you cite something from an expert's book, you are able to borrow the credibility of that author. Knowing that you now have their years of experience behind you lends you greater self-assurance and fortifies you mentally.

Imagine that you are leading a team discussion about how to integrate some Internet- based software, such as a CRM program, into your company's operations and you're able to make a powerful statement such as, "We've been analyzing various technology options to make us more effective, and I've been reading Bill Gates' book, *Business at the Speed of Thought*. It addresses how the implementation of instantaneous electronic hardware, software, and communications technology has revolutionized the operational speed of so many cutting-edge companies such as Microsoft, Google, and Amazon. When I read his vision, it brought to mind some ways that similar systems and strategies can help make our operation way more effective too."

With a statement like that, you've just brought the power and authority of Bill Gates and Microsoft (one of the most innovative men and companies in history) into your meeting, thereby influencing your teams' attitudes toward the changes you are proposing and lending greater credibility to you and your plan. Exposing yourself to the wisdom of experts and incorporating it into your own plans prepares you for, and even reduces, the prospect of negative pushback. Listeners know that you did your homework and that you did it with more than just a specialist—you did it with a master. If someone wants to push back now, they are not just pushing back against you, they are also pushing back against Bill Gates. Acquiring wisdom and credibility by reading what experts have written raises your mental toughness quotient considerably and does it a lot faster than if you had to spend years learning by experience alone.

The second reason why reading is so effective is that there is no ego involved. It's just you and the expert's thoughts on the page. You can teach yourself in a *bare-naked* way. Now that I got your attention, let me clarify: I mean *ego* naked, not *body* naked. You are the one person your ego will allow you to get completely naked with. It's automatic and extremely enlightening. When you read, your ego gets out of the way and lowers all of the mental barriers you may have with others. As you access expertise from a book and run it through your head to process it, you are coaching yourself with that expert's wisdom. You can be totally honest because you know your weaknesses, but you don't have to reveal them to anyone else. Reading allows you to open up and just absorb without having to make any impressions or engage with others. In that protected space, you are able to learn and allow that expert to be your personal coach. That kind of coaching raises your mental toughness quotient substantially.

I must say that my own mental toughness has grown and improved greatly from my ongoing reading and study of capitalism and how it applies to American history as well as to American business's continuing success. In the introduction of his book *How Capitalism Will Save Us*, Steve Forbes talks about the iPod economy and how much of a bad rap capitalism and private enterprise get from much of the media, college educators, and even, at times, from uber successful business people such as Warren Buffet, who believes prosperity has been disproportionately rewarding to people like himself. Forbes discusses how his book was written, in part, because Americans are no longer taught how capitalism and free enterprise really work, and he wanted to help educate people in a conversational way so that they would understand what "democratic capitalism" really is. He also wanted them to know why it is by far the best system in the world for turning scarcity into abundance anywhere it is implemented. That book was written in 2009 at the end of a giant economic meltdown and was updated in 2011. Today the public onslaught against capitalism has grown stronger on college campuses and now even among members of Congress and the Senate, going all the way up to presidential candidates.

Even though the attempts of socialism have failed dismally across the globe, concepts of socialism grow stronger in America every election cycle. Socialism has consistently produced abysmal economies. Although there are a few socialist and communist countries whose economies have grown—largely due to population growth—those countries continually gravitate towards the practice of some free enterprise, allowing more elements of capitalism to develop within their system. It would seem that in America—the very bedrock of capitalism—that sheer common sense would have us all advancing and promoting the benefits of capitalism instead of socialism. To be clear, this book on Rugged Entrepreneurialism is not a special promotion of capitalism; it is a book about what it takes to be a Rugged Entrepreneur. That said, having a capitalistic free enterprise system sure makes entrepreneurial success a lot more possible.

Reading and discussing books that teach us all about the power of capitalism and business ownership is important for having the mental toughness to contend with an ever-growing sentiment against those with great aspirations in our country. All entrepreneurs have to be mentally tough enough to deal with that portion of American culture that is anti-business and anti-capitalism. You also have to strengthen your understanding of the roots of American business success and be proud of that continuing success. By merely attempting to be a successful entrepreneur, you join a small percentage of the population (about 10 to 14 percent) who look to succeed as business owners. We will address this topic further in chapter seven, which covers drive and purpose, because having a proper education on capitalism is a very important part of constructing a solid Rugged foundation. Unfortunately, not all entrepreneurs know that.

Having the right foundation, being resolute in your purpose, and having the mental toughness to educate others about capitalism, its benefits, and your choice to personally exercise it, are crucial. I emphasize this because many in that group of people who are not trying to succeed in a business of their own (that is 85 to 90 percent of the population), will see your unique move as something that shines an unwelcome light on their relative lack of desire or grit to build something they own. While it is not your intention, it happens. Some of those people will bombard you with negativity that you have to be tough enough to deal with. To start creating the right foundation, I strongly recommend that you read two books: *How Capitalism Saved America* by Thomas DiLorenzo and the aforementioned *How Capitalism Will Save Us* by Steve Forbes. They will enhance your understanding of why capitalism *and* mental toughness is so important.

Twenty years ago, Daphene and I were asked to speak to a group of several thousand business owners about the mindset it takes to succeed in business for oneself and the systems that can help support that endeavor. We were slated to be the warm-up speakers, and the keynote guest at the event was Steve Forbes, the editor-in-chief of *Forbes* magazine who was, at that time, also seeking the nomination to become the Republican candidate for president of the United States. Although Mr. Forbes had not yet written his book *How Capitalism Will Save Us*, meeting him on that occasion led me to purchase and read it when it was published. That book then became the catalyst for me to read *How Capitalism Saved America* and countless other books to follow. I give a lot of credit to both works for helping me become mentally tougher and passionate about promoting capitalism, free enterprise, and ultimately, formulating and teaching Rugged Entrepreneurialism.

Do you have a reading regime? If not, I suggest immediately creating one. I am still an avid reader to this day, but for the fifteen-year period when I was doing a deep study on leadership in general, and on American leadership more specifically, I was a voracious reader. I was also studying entrepreneurial history and embarking on my own spiritual journey. I intentionally read one to two books a month on the subjects I was pursuing expertise in, and of course, I always made room on my list for other books by authors whom I greatly respected for their proven accomplishments. I didn't just gloss over these books. I learned to read them with a highlighter, a pen, and a bookmark in hand. I highlighted anything that caught my attention. I added notes to those highlighted sections when rereading them or if something came to mind that was instantly applicable to some area of my personal or business life. After finishing the book, I would go back and reread those sections and notes to see if they sparked even more thoughts. That education was ten times more valuable to me than my college degree because I was passionate about what I was studying and instantly applied much of what I was learning to the relevant aspects of my life.

"A" for Associating: Obviously, reading is a form of positive association if the material is beneficial and from a credible source, but the kind of associations I am referring to here are the in-person kind, where ideas are exchanged and relationships are formed. Many experts say that the people you physically associate with and the books you read make a huge impact on your life and career. Some even believe that it dictates who and where you will be in a three- to five-year time period.

I agree with these experts and would even add that association is the factor that can have the biggest pendulum effect on your mental toughness quotient. Unlike reading, which allows you to grow the fastest and has almost no downside, some associations can be excellent for your mental toughness while others can be damaging. Who you choose to associate with makes all the difference in the world. Your choices can sway the outcome either way. I often remind the people who work in our organizations that knowing who *not* to associate with and be influenced by, can be as important as knowing who to associate with. Let's look more closely at the healthy side of the association swing.

In sports almost everyone knows that practicing with and playing with people who are better, stronger, and faster than you are will make you better too. They also know that the reverse is true. Playing with people far less skilled than you can keep you stagnant, or worse, set you back a pace. Ruggeds develop an instinct for telling the two types of people apart and for gravitating toward associations with people in life and business who are bigger, better, faster, and stronger than they are. When Ruggeds associate with those greater than them, they are forced to work and communicate on the same level. Although it may be a stretch at first, they intuitively know that the effort is worth it. This kind of association presents an opportunity to see and study things that will make them better. Holding their own in these circumstances forces humility on them, but it also develops mental toughness.

I remember the feeling and the results well. In the humble second year of building the model for our company's mattress and furniture business, we were invited to a major industry dinner. To give you an indication of where our company was in its development, this was well before we came up with the name BoxDrop™. We were still a licensed hub-satellite model that we called Local Furniture Direct! My personal industry coach and expert advisory board member, Bob O'Neil, had been hosting this particular dinner for some thirty years. When extending the invitation to us, he actually told me that I needed to attend so that I could see what it was like to wear "big boy buying pants." Bob is a legendary sales executive and Rugged Entrepreneur in the home furnishings industry who has spent a lifetime investing in relationships throughout that world. Among the leaders who regularly attended this biannual event were furniture industry expert investment banker Jerry Epperson of Mann, Armistead, & Epperson; E.J. and Randy Strelitz, who own and run The Dump, which is a chain of huge furniture stores extending across the country in high population markets; Eric Easter, the president of Kittles, a large regional chain of furniture stores in Indiana; representatives from *Furniture Today,* the industry's leading business publication; and a few other very successful retail furniture business owners.

Bob knew that the association would stretch us, and he also knew that it would expose us to the wisdom of others who had built businesses ahead of us that were far bigger than we were. Being stretched like this helps open your mind to what can be. It makes you hungry to find a way to play better, faster, and harder. Bob let me know that it was a biannual dinner, to which we would be invited to attend at every High Point market. Being able to associate with such accomplished industry people and knowing that we would get the opportunity to do so on repeat basis was a great motivator. While you are forced to accept your humble position during a first interaction like that, you are also compelled to choose how you want to be perceived the next time you see these players. Will you stay at that same level and feel less than significant again next year? Or will you put the knowledge you gather in their company to good use and come back closer to being an equal? The right kind of uncomfortable association can provide incredible motivation and momentum.

Bear in mind that being the small guy at the table requires humility and mental toughness just to hold your own. Even if you struggle to keep up at first, it's encouraging to know that when you return the next time, you will be more prepared than the first time. Associations that demand you stretch yourself will help raise your mental toughness quotient exponentially. They drive you to overcome fear, check your ego, focus your thoughts, and play catch up. Because the others know you are the little guy, they openly share secrets of their success. If you are smart and wish to truly rise to their level, you will soak up what they say like a sponge!

By the time we returned for our ninth dinner five years later, our company had grown by triple digits almost every year and had been ranked in the top 20 percent of fastest growing privately held companies on *Inc.* magazine's Inc. 5000 list two years in a row. As of the publication of this book, Retail Service System's BoxDrop™ Mattress & Furniture model has opened over 450 locations in 47 states. The RSS team is also off to a very successful launch of a first market mover and an exciting new franchise with bioPURE™ Service, which began long before the COVID-19 crisis. What a difference five years can make, especially when you allow yourself to associate with people who make you uncomfortable in ways that push you to do better. In fact, **Associating with Others Who Make You Feel Uncomfortable** should be added to the list of things a Rugged does that a navel-gazer would never even consider doing.

Another great way for entrepreneurs to make associations work in their favor is by creating an advisory board. I mentioned the value of such boards before, but it bears repeating. You must approach these associations with deep respect and appreciation for the potential wisdom they offer. You must also assure members that they can speak their mind with you. Why would anyone not want an advisory board? It gives you access to other great minds. Early in my entrepreneurial career I didn't have or really know I could create one. As I became more passionate about reading and studying leadership, I learned about the concept of "mastermind groups" in a story from Napoleon Hill's book *Think and Grow Rich*. The concept made perfect sense to me, and I coined it for my business-building purposes as "Mastermind Teams."

The story, as I remember it, was about how Henry Ford had taken a local newspaper to court over their reporting that he was not very bright. It was claimed that Ford was far too ignorant to have been the creator of many of the products that his automotive company built. While presenting his case, Ford pointed to a team of engineers who were present in the courtroom and said that while he might not have been able to build a certain engine on his own, but he was the one who had the idea to assemble the "mastermind group" that did. Thank God for finding that gem while reading a book. That one story is the primary reason I devoted myself to becoming an incredible team builder, which is now one of my greatest strengths as a Rugged.

Once you understand how valuable association is, you not only start using it to improve yourself, but soon you use it build teams. Before you know it, the mastermind team concept is an integral part of your company. It is now in its DNA. Whether team members know it or not, their associations with one another foster a healthy dose of friendly, creative competition that helps the whole organization succeed. When an organization has that kind of combined energy, it creates a momentum that elevates everyone and builds a better overall culture. People in our organizations are eager to be on our mastermind teams and once they are on one, they want to contribute. Regional and national leaders emerge from those teams because they're able to show that they can inspire, influence decisions, pull together ideas, and produce results. You can see how well someone operates when they are in a team. It is quickly evident whether they are navel-gazers, frozen by "detailitis," or a possible Rugged leader. The mastermind culture provides a practical testing ground for leadership qualities. It is a powerful tool to use for disrupting an industry or scaling an organization at a rapid pace.

In creating my advisory board for Retail Service Systems, I set out to build a stellar mastermind team. I asked three of the most serious Rugged Entrepreneurs I knew to participate. Bob O'Neill, whom I mentioned earlier, is a career furniture industry expert who was on the original board for the World Furniture Market in Las Vegas and ultimately sold his company to Leggett & Platt and continued running it as a division of that company before retiring. He then returned to the business of being a Rugged by starting a closeout network that is one of *the* largest in the industry. Marty Traber is a Vietnam veteran who became the lead securities attorney for one of the largest law firms in America, and along the way helped start a publicly traded New York Stock Exchange insurance company. He retired at seventy-two years of age (that's when I asked him to join our advisory board) in order to start and be the chairman of a boutique investment bank out of Tampa Florida called Skyway Capital. And last, but not least, Dewey Andrew is a Rugged who had a brief stint in professional sports before entering sales, becoming an entrepreneur in the distribution industry, and building a multibrand, multimillion-dollar company that he sold to become a venture capitalist. He now owns part of several hotels, real estate developments, and golf courses, and sits on the board of a large pharmaceutical company. In addition to being my father and great friend, he is someone with whom I love talking business.

Details about this extraordinary advisory board and their influence are scattered throughout this book, but from the brief descriptions of each member provided here, you can see that it is a board whose involvement not only stretches me and our executive team, but stretches everyone else in our companies who directly or indirectly associates with them.

Naturally, I had to have a humble enough spirit to ask people of this caliber to challenge us. When faced with the same daunting task, you might feel like you cannot possibly ask this of someone. Or you may be afraid they will say no. But overcoming that fear is a part of building mental toughness. When you do finally make your request, let them know that the arrangement is not tied to a fixed amount of time or set schedule. Assure them that they can participate by phone or email and at *their* convenience. If you ask the right type of person, they will see it as an honor. But you have to mean it, and you have to allow them into your personal and business house in order to get their open, honest opinion about what you have planned and how you intend to carry it out.

A true desire to be advised yields a type of association that benefits you on multiple levels. In the same way that reading a great book extends the credibility and authority of its author to you, so does an association with expert advisors. When you have the right type of advisory board mentoring you and your team with their wisdom, they buy into your company, offer indispensable advice, connect you to their sphere of influence, and open doors that would normally have taken you years to open by yourself. The collective credibility of this advisory board becomes an inherent part of yours and your organization's credibility. The more experienced and respected they are, the better it is for you and your team. Are you too prideful to ask successful people for help? Or are you mentally tough enough to make that leap?

Ruggeds look to associate with like-minded and positive people who challenge us to grow and improve as much as we possibly can. This is true in our personal lives as well as in our business lives. Insofar as every association has the potential to impact your mind, it is wise to surround yourself with the best associates. Positive ones strengthen your mental toughness and are also fun to be around.

Negative associations, on the other hand, can be very detrimental. These are people who feed off unnecessary drama in their life. Their focus on the negative produces what my wife and I call "drama bombs." Negative associates also tend to have a victim mentality. We describe these people as "emotional vampires" because they will literally drain creative and productive energy from you. The more you feed them, the hungrier they get.

When you encounter these negative influences, remember that they are soul-suckers. The use of the word "vampire" is intentional. The word should trigger your mental toughness to keep them away. Ruggeds need to be productive. They do not have time to feed the insatiable appetites of troublesome people. The more mentally tough you are, the easier it is to keep them at bay. As you separate yourself from those negative associations you will find that you have a lot more time for positive and productive people. You will also find that you spend more mental time working on solving your own challenges instead of attending to theirs, which are almost always highly exaggerated and never-ending.

In today's world of social media, almost every business has connections through platforms such as Facebook, Twitter, LinkedIn, and Instagram. You must approach these platforms in the same spirit as you approach assembling an advisory board. There is only room and time enough for positive associations. You can make many wonderful connections through this medium, but you must also guard against the negative ones. This is especially true if you do not have any direct knowledge whether the person is successful as an entrepreneur or not. Some negative influences are analogous to the anonymous people who write stupid things on bathroom walls. In many ways, they treat social media and the Internet like one giant bathroom stall door. When you don't know if someone on a given platform is failing or succeeding in life or business, you don't know if they have good intentions or bad. Sadly, I've witnessed too many entrepreneurs unwittingly follow Rugged wannabes on social media. Beware of imposters. They are not good associates. Many of these faux Ruggeds want to feel better about themselves. Rather than be alone in their unhappiness and failure, they position themselves as knowing more than they do, or as knowing more than others, hoping to get followers. We have all heard that misery loves company. It's an expression that's been around for ages because it is often true, and the same can be said for failure. No failing entrepreneur wants to be in that category alone. If you choose to associate directly or indirectly with people who are negative, misleading, or failing, you will surely weaken your mental toughness. In fact, the fastest way to reduce your MTQ is by associating with people who are no longer trying to win and who don't want you to win either. You will find a small percentage of such people in every large organization, from sport groups, to religious, business, and social groups, and, of course, online. Every large group that we have built or been a part of has always revealed a vampire or two or ten .... They are typically envious of others having leadership roles or jealous of those succeeding when they are not. Developing the mental toughness to stay away from those influences or to remove them from your team is crucial.

Let's return for a moment to the notion of a pendulum effect, which we discussed earlier.

I'd like to clarify the concept by using a metaphorical story in true Rugged Intellect style. Imagine yourself as a business journeyman who is traveling toward a destination named Success and to towns beyond called Better Success and Best Success. The path to Success has been traveled by others, and they have compiled maps and hired guides to help anyone who wishes to get there too. They offer these maps and guides through their company, Good Guides Inc. Good Guides receives a monetary and pride benefit every time someone uses their maps and guides, so you could say that Good Guides has a vested interest in you reaching Success. Good Guides only hires guides who have made it to Success and the towns beyond safely themselves. To ensure your smooth travel, the maps note all the pitfalls prior adventurers headed to Success encountered so you can avoid those same traps.

While you are on this journey, you realize that you also have access to several free guides via group associations and social media. Some of the creators of these free guides say they've made it to Success before and some do not, but you really have no way of confirming this. Many of them may have failed or are failing now for any number of reasons you cannot see, such as sudden illness, substance abuse, shortage of funds, bad spending choices, distractions in their personal life, or just because they are navel-gazers who always think they know better. Some could have failed to get to Success or beyond because of "excuse-itis," laziness, or unwittingly accepting advice from people who never made it to Success either. Very little is known about these free guides except that a lot of them complain on social media about Good Guides. Some of them say that they had a Good Guide before, but he or she didn't help them when times got tough or when they got stuck.

The journey to Success and beyond can follow multiple trails and present many challenges, such as inclement weather, path erosion, fallen trees, collapsed bridges, or damaged river crossings, to say nothing of predatory animals. When you access the Good Guides maps you are always accessing the knowledge of people who have made it past all of those obstacles. By contrast, when you access any number of the free guides, you cannot be sure that the information they are passing along isn't just hearsay. Maybe the creators of these free guides have never been on the path but have only heard about it. Maybe they took it partway and turned back when things got tough. Or maybe they got stuck and are hoping that someone will join them to get them out of their predicament.

The Good Guides humbly admit that they got stuck from time to time but are proud that they made it to Success and the towns beyond. They want you to get there as well because it builds their credibility, adds another success story to the Good Guide Inc. history, and benefits them financially. The Good Guides are measured not only by how many journeymen they get to Success and beyond, but how fast they get them there, and by how many customers continue to travel on to further destinations, including Better Success and Best Success.

As you navigate the Rugged terrain to Success yourself, you will have many questions. The trip will not always be as easy as you thought it would be. Under these conditions you may even dismiss your Good Guides' directions and turn to free guides for alternate advice. (Remember, when something is free, it is usually a good indication of its worth.) If you do seek the help of free guides, you will hear them say such things as: I am better than the Good Guides, I am smarter than the Good Guides, the Good Guides are ripping you off, the Good Guides don't really understand you, the Good Guides are keeping secrets from you, I just want to help you, I know how to get to Success faster than the Good Guides, and so forth.

How do you know if the free guides can deliver what they promise? Can you compare their number of satisfied customers to those of the Good Guides? If Good Guides has helped several hundred and has a visible following and the free guides don't advertise how many people they've helped or have a visible following, those free guides are likely misleading you. Do the free guides have a vested interest in your success? If not, they are likely to get you off-track from your mission to get to Success and beyond (also known as, becoming a true Rugged Entrepreneur).

On the real journey, Ruggeds create opportunities to associate with Good Guides, and sometimes they find themselves with the free or questionable ones. How far do you think the pendulum would swing if you were the journeyman who stumbled on the path to success because you made a wrong choice of associates? Your best protection against this prospect is to develop your Rugged Intellect, which includes being intuitive enough to spot these negative influences before they steer you wrong. You must be mentally tough enough to push them away if they get too close.

The first time I witnessed this kind of negative dynamic was in college where approximately 41 percent of entrants fail to earn a degree. I warn you, the easiest way for a college freshman to join the ranks of those who never earn a diploma is by associating with upperclassmen who are on their way out. I graduated college in four years with a pretty good GPA and was fortunate enough to hitch my wagon to some older students who were ambitious enough to have a plan and to work hard. One of my three suitemates during my freshman year was not as fortunate. He got caught up with some sophomores who loved to party. Before long he was skipping classes, going out three or four nights a week, and playing pick up sports with them instead of studying. By the end of the year, he was packing up to head home, never to return to campus again.

I observed some of the same bad choices during my junior and senior years in college after I had joined a fraternity. It is a great fraternity with a diverse group of brothers. There were plenty of intramural athletic teams, study groups, advisors, officers, parties, charitable events, and many other options to keep us busy without distracting us from our studies. Although the brothers had a common bond and pledged to look after one another, there was always a group of failing brothers who were all too quick to pull a younger brother or pledge into their lair. Before you knew it, that new brother was on the path to failure, just like the older counterparts.

David Wilson, who is now a co-owner in bioPURE™, the chief marketing officer both for bioPURE™ and BoxDrop™, as well as an owner in and the CMO of our mass media network Rugged ETV (The Rugged Nation Network), was a year ahead of me in that fraternity. He and a few others who were officers in the fraternity took me under their wing. Because of those positive associations, I learned how to study better and to look for leadership opportunities in the fraternity and in the national fraternal organization. Their influence led me to becoming the fraternity's proconsul, a student senator at NC State my senior year, and also to learning how to be a better interviewer and resume builder when it came time to get my first job.

David always amazed me because he was number one in his class and he knew that he wanted to go straight to graduate school and earn his masters degree in business at the University of North Carolina Chapel Hill after graduation. He also knew that he would go to work for one of the leading consulting companies in the country right after that. From there, he intended to find a path to be an entrepreneur. He became one of my best friends and an extremely positive influence on me for many years. Again, my first real business startup was the sales circular/ newspaper he and I formed during my senior year at NC State and his first year at graduate school. Today he is a Rugged Entrepreneur who has helped found and grow multiple businesses, one of which was sold for more than a hundred million dollars. I often think of some of my pledge brothers, including those who came after me. Some, whom I positively influenced the same way as others positively influenced me, went on to enjoy success. Several, though, chose to associate with the partiers and flunked out. How much of the fun they had with bad associates do they regret now? Do they realize how those associations impacted their life all the way up to today?

"I" Is for Investing: Investment has many implications in our acrostic for increasing your mental toughness quotient.

First, it indicates that you absolutely must develop an investment mentality about raising your mental toughness quotient. You simply have to put in the time, energy, and resources to see it grow.

Second, an investment is usually a serious undertaking. You are giving something of value to get something of greater value. You cannot squander the opportunity.

Last, one only invests in something when they believe it has the potential to be of high value. The word "investing" here suggests that your mental toughness has the potential to be one of your greatest assets.

With ongoing contributions, this asset can grow exponentially. An investment in your own mental toughness can yield truly great returns. Essentially, the stock value of mental toughness cannot be underestimated. Any increase in its value can improve the worth of a Rugged, and the worth of his or her business.

This entire R.A.I.S.E.M.E. acrostic offers ways for you to invest in your mental toughness so I will not repeat them here. Some of them involve monetary investments, but most are about the investment of time and ingenuity.

As already noted, reading involves an investment of money to buy books and an investment of time to read and absorb their wisdom. Associating with positive influences requires an investment of money to share a meal or to buy a gift of appreciation, or possibly to offer a bonus to advisory board members, and, of course, it requires the investment of time and reflection. These are relatively small investments for such enormous ROI (return on investment).

"S" Is for Surrounding: We've certainly touched upon the subject of "Surrounding" when we discussed mental toughness and the importance of being around people you can learn from, but Surrounding, as it applies to your environment, is a favorite and unique part of this acrostic because it reflects a neat hobby I have. It is a hobby that has grown as my success has grown. I'm not only a collector of aphorisms, quotes, and parables, or, as I collectively call them, word-picture stories, I am also an avid collector of objects that inspire me. If you work in an office, or even multiple offices as I do, I believe you should surround yourself with such things. They provide constant motivation. All of the offices in my homes, workplaces, and headquarters contain keepsakes that galvanize me. My wife considers these decorated spaces the neatest rooms in whichever of our homes or buildings they are located. They are like eclectic museums combining old and new objects, many of which are connected to our businesses, friendships, and family histories. Collectibles, works of art, sports memorabilia, war- and history-related pieces that recognize and commemorate people, places, and events of global importance, favorite books, pictures, particularly of Daff and me with people we've grown to admire, met, and studied—you name it, and you'll find it there. It's a big energetic assortment that relays important stories, holds heroic history, builds pride, and inspires greatness. Above all, it is designed to help me maintain a grateful, inquisitive, and creative attitude about developing and building things.

When I was a junior in college at North Carolina State University, the then-president of our fraternity (Sigma Chi) was a great young man named Mike Wallace. Mike was the kind of leader who represented himself and the fraternity well. His demeanor was a nice blend of humor and seriousness. While he was earning his degree, he worked for an agency that contracted with local grocery stores to collect on bad checks. The business was owned by a sharp young entrepreneur who trusted Mike with the keys to his office, which was only a few miles from campus in downtown Raleigh. He also allowed Mike to work whatever random evening and weekend hours he wanted. They had created a great system for contacting and tracking communications even though everything was done by hand in those days, as we were still in the floppy disk stage of computing.

Mike was planning his transition into full-time work after graduation and knew he would be leaving that job behind. Looking to take care of the business owner and also looking to give a younger fraternity brother an opportunity, he told me about it and asked if I would be interested. I was ambitious and responsible, and I also wanted to earn extra money so a flexible job on top of the one I already had, with good pay sounded great to me. Mike took me to the office one evening and introduced me to the owner, whose name was Neil, and then spent the next few hours showing me the system and how to call and deal with the people whose checks had bounced. I agreed to the job, and we set up a time for me to come back and go over everything with Neil. When I returned, Neil pointed out a mirror on his office wall and explained to me that smiling when you are speaking on the phone to customers is very effective. The mirror was there for me to double-check from time to time and be sure that I was doing that. He told me that it helps to have a congenial manner when handling a challenging situation with people who were sometimes very frustrated.

That lesson never left me and the job itself was great training. It also helped me during an internship I did my senior year with E.F. Hutton. Since that time, I've come across the same advice in a Zig Ziglar book and have always kept a mirror somewhere in each of my offices to remind me to smile as much as possible in all communications. The mirror is one of those important and inspiring objects in my surroundings that I mentioned earlier. Various historic items from my grandparents, as well as pictures, prints, and paintings that make me reflect, are also on my office walls. *Two Indian Horses* by the artist Bev Doolittle and a print of *The Son of Man* by René Magritte are ones that remind me to meditate and work on my vision skills. They both invite you to think about the things you may miss even though they are right in front of you, and about the things that are beyond the obvious. Surrounding yourself with images that help you focus, remind you of your responsibilities, fill you with pride, and make you thankful will inspire you every day.

Aside from some very important books that changed my life incredibly, the most treasured piece in any of my offices is a small handwrought steel hammer. Daff had opened an R & D test store to develop methods for what—after a few gritty years of trial and error— ultimately became the the first BoxDrop™ store. At the time, we had an advertising and merchandising idea that involved us ordering some furniture close-out containers from various manufacturers for that test store named RSSCO Outlets. When those containers arrived, she and I unloaded them ourselves. It was an awesome experience as the containers were giant boxes filled with a surprise mix of different furnishings that also came in boxes. After we unloaded the container, we chose some bedroom and dining room sets to place on the showroom floor. Typically, when you open a case goods box, you will find a small plastic bag of parts, tools, and assembly instructions that the manufacturers supply for you. The dining room table box we had opened that day contained an item that didn't look at all like those standard tools. It was a small handmade steel hammer with cheesecloth wrapped around its handle. I knew immediately that it must have belonged to one of the Vietnamese workers who pieced together some of the furniture before packing it.

In Asia, many of the factories employ thousands of workers who live on the plant site for ten months out of the year. Theirs is challenging work that often involves several generations of family members laboring together. I could picture an older Vietnamese man using that handmade hammer for twenty years or more. He had clearly left that important tool in the box accidentally. It was now my good fortune to receive it. It remains in my office to this day and is one of my life's great treasures. I keep it on a wall with some other Retail Service Systems, BoxDrop™, BioPURE™, and Rugged Entrepreneurial memorabilia. It reminds me of how thankful I am to have been born in America. My opportunities here are based on common law, private ownership, and free enterprise capitalism, while that hardworking Vietnamese man very likely grew up poor, working in a factory from an early age, very far from his home village, with little chance for upward mobility. I could never say thank you enough for having the blessing of being born in America as opposed to being born in a one-party socialist republic whose political and economic systems offer far less potential for Rugged Entrepreneurs.

In addition to being a unique piece that would inspire appreciation as an office decoration, that hammer became a great "thought seed." That highly appreciated gift was "dropped" accidentally in a dining room set "box" and was subsequently loaded with a lot of other boxes into a large container. The large shipping container, which is a big steel box itself, was ultimately "dropped" off at Daff's R & D store and became the seed for us naming the new business model BoxDrop. The name has become an iconic national success and another great RSS war story.

I suspect that the cheesecloth wrapped around the handle of that hammer provided very little comfort to the weathered and calloused hand of the person who wielded it day in and day out. Having that hammer on my wall moves me to do my best in business, to utilize my God-given skills, to appreciate my opportunities, and to do something great with them. It also reminds me that my passion and mission, which is now Retail Service Systems' mission, is to "Empower Entrepreneurs." Daff and I have committed our lives to building business success, mentoring business pioneers, and promoting and teaching free enterprise capitalism and Rugged Entrepreneurialism everywhere we can.

Surrounding yourself with anything that makes a big impact on your daily attitude and gratitude will make whatever tasks you are working on go that much better. To the extent that it is affordable, it is also important to create inspirational work environments for your teams and organizations. Helping your people feel creative and inspired at work is a great advantage to Rugged organizations disrupting the marketplace. At Retail Service Systems headquarters in Dublin, Ohio, we have an entire office building dedicated to "Empowering Entrepreneurs." Before one even walks in the door, they are greeted with a sign reading just that. This sign sets the tone for how everyone on our team approaches the day, *every* day. It also sends a message to any vendor or manufacturing partners who come to visit us. It tells them exactly what our mission is so that they can focus on ways to help us empower our Rugged Entrepreneur customers too. Amy Bowen, who is RSS's controller, and Jill Smith, her assistant, have completely decorated the office space, prominently displaying all of the company's awards and news stories covering our Rugged success. Everywhere you look there is some reminder of the teams' mission to empower entrepreneurs.

Never underestimate the dynamic effect of creating mission-centric surroundings. The turnover rate among key employees at Retail Service Systems during its first six years of triple digit growth was almost zero. We only lost one of those key people to a company that recruited him in the hopes that he could help them duplicate our energy and community. People within our organizations—particularly those working on a customer service level—report that they love our creative, mission-centric surroundings. It provides a daily reminder that what they do matters and makes a difference in the lives of others. The supportive and optimistic atmosphere also helps our organization develop talent from within, inspiring good team members to become great team members.

As emphasized in the "Associate" section of this chapter, surrounding yourself with great people, as we have committed ourselves to doing, is even more important than surrounding yourself with an inspirational environment. When building an employee team that works together in the same space, those people are also an important part of the surroundings. You must measure and try to pick positive, teachable people who will work well with others. That said, an inspirational working environment that promotes a positive energy and mission can help stave off what is often referred to as "the crabs in a bucket problem."

There is an observation about crabs in a bucket that is often shared in books on winning and having a positive attitude. I will share it here in case you haven't encountered it before, as it bears an important message, though my version has a bit of a twist.

When you put one crab in a bucket, just like a spider, it can easily find a way to climb up and out. However, when you put a handful of crabs in a bucket, no crabs can escape because every crab attempting to get to the top will be grabbed by another that will pull it back down into the bucket.

What other business books often miss in this story is that we are *people,* not crabs, and people have free will. They are not captured and forced in a bucket against their will. If you choose to be in a bucket with a bunch of crabs, then the blame is on you. You selected your surroundings. You are responsible for being alongside of those negative crabs clawing at others, making excuses for their failures, seeing problems where they don't exist, overdramatizing them, and murmuring about the successful people with hard-enough shells and the determination to get out. The dramatic end to the crab story that is often omitted is this:

Over time, the crabs poop in the bucket, pee in the bucket, spit in the bucket, sweat in the bucket, and spill the blood of their companions in the bucket as crabs often do. A few crabs die in the bucket, and their rotting carcasses add to the stagnant nasty, toxic, poisonous swill that builds up in the bottom of the bucket. The swill turns the crabs green with envy, softens their shells, leaving them defenseless until they can no longer make even the feeblest attempt to get out of the bucket. Business leaders who do not build great environments often allow "crabs" in a bucket atmosphere to foster and are thus likely doomed to failure.

Now, how important do you think your surroundings and the people you choose to be part of your teams and environments are?

"E" Is for Entertaining: Ruggeds enjoy entertainment and an occasional escape as all people do. Some people, however, spend almost as much time being entertained or trying to escape work as they spend on work itself. On one hand, this is tragically sad, but on the other, it represents an awesome opportunity for us Ruggeds. While those people are otherwise engaged, Ruggeds are busy entertaining themselves by investing in their own development. They are wisely putting their time into increasing their mental toughness quotient. You may react to that by thinking, *I'm old enough or even successful enough that changing my entertainment habits isn't necessary to protect or grow my mental toughness.* But Warren Buffet, one of the world's wealthiest billionaires, would disagree. At eighty-eight years of age, Buffet spends a large amount of his day reading and regularly playing competitive bridge. In a 2017 *Washington Post* interview, Buffet told a reporter that he played at least four sessions of bridge a week and that each session averaged about two hours. On a *CNBC Squawk Box* interview in February 2019, Buffet said he holds a slight edge in bridge over one of his favorite competitors, Bill Gates, who has been ranked as the world's wealthiest person almost every year between 1995 to 2018. Buffet says that he loves bridge because it keeps him sharp.

Gates and Buffet believe that playing bridge fuels a competitive spirit and forces them to think because there are so many different things to contemplate. In his own words, Buffet says, *"You can play a hand every six or seven minutes every day for the rest of your life, and you will never see the same hand ... " "You are seeing a different intellectual challenge every seven minutes."* Any simple Google search on the subject of these two icons and their bridge-playing sessions will yield several articles, video clips, and stories about their love of the game. In one YouTube video promoting bridge to the youth of the world, Bill Gates calls it a sport and says that anyone who is good at bridge will be good at a lot of other things. See https://www.youtube.com/watch?v=nJcFspR5koc.

There are a number of competitive sports where you can invest time to keep your mind keen, and several of them also help you stay in great physical shape. The point of this is to encourage you to work mental toughness training into your entertainment activities as often as you possibly can. If you want to play golf, do it with associates who want to raise your and their mental toughness as much as they want to play the game. Whenever you can, also turn your entertainment time into time that exercises your *business* mind. Mark Cuban was so serious about this that he bought the Dallas Mavericks. Now he's not just a passionate NBA fan, he's also an NBA franchise owner! It's the perfect merger of business and pleasure. He is so invested in both that the temper and passion he directs toward the referees at games is legendary. In 2018, when I was invited to attend a Jaguars game with the owner, Shahid Khan, I also witnessed this perfect merger of business and entertainment. Khan's love of the sport not only led him to buy the team, it also led him to invest in building up and revitalizing Jacksonville's downtown waterfront district. Do you suppose that cultivating his mental toughness while mixing his passions for entertainment and business had anything to do with Shahid Khan's success? I do. You've got to love both to grow the value of a team from the seven hundred and sixty million he paid for it, to more than two billion dollars over the first five years he owned the Jaguars.

Think about all of the different elements a professional team owner must contend with, from the team's general management, the stadium's management, and talent and coaching management, to the business of entertainment and revenue sharing on merchandise. It all requires injecting your mental toughness into the organization.

Throughout my studies of Rugged Millionaires verses Rugged Billionaires, I've noted that one of the greatest differences between the two groups is how much more billionaires tend to build additional business enterprises around their personal entertainment interests.

Numerous billionaires have secondary business interests in forms of entertainment that they love because they are happy to invest their skills in improving those mediums even more.

I am not saying a Rugged has to create a connection between business and entertainment; I am just saying that the more one ties those things together, the more they raise their mental toughness quotient and the value of their favorite entertainment as well. On the surface, Daff's and my personal entertainment choices seem less business-related than these other examples. For instance, we enjoy playing pickle ball together, walking our dogs, and watching movies. But because my wife and I build our business enterprises together, we often talk about those businesses when we're out on our walks. We also have a passion for football both at the college and pro levels, so over the last ten years we intentionally connected this form of sports entertainment to our business-building efforts. It started with us creating an internship program. We first hired college athletes for various summer jobs to help them learn business skills while we benefited from the connection between our companies and various popular sports in our markets. One of our favorite experiences involved Zac Brooks, a star running back at Clemson University. Zac worked for Daff at our first super BoxDrop™ research and development test store in Anderson, South Carolina, during the summer of 2015, following his junior season. He had worked hard, had a great smile, and had an awesome attitude. When he returned to school for his senior year, he set us up with a grand tour of the new Clemson facilities and arranged for us to meet coaches and to see the inside of the program. We were invited to games and grew very connected to the Clemson Tiger community in a way that made us feel as if we were more than fans. The awesome fun of tying our business interests together with a form of entertainment we absolutely love continued when Zac was picked in the 2016 NFL draft to play for the Seattle Seahawks alongside one of our favorite North Carolina State graduates, Russell Wilson. Today, Clemson football is a customer of one of our company's bioPURE™ Services, and it is a very important part of our mission to change the world's view of clean. Their use of our services also makes a statement about how much Clemson values the well-being of its players and program.

In recent years, our combined love of football and work extended even further, this time connecting us with the Jacksonville Jaguars and the NFL. Our vice president and chief community officer, Darren Conrad, lived in Jacksonville, Florida, and thus was quite familiar with the dynamic growth the city and their resident NFL team were experiencing. Our organization was looking to build a national training and distribution center for some time and this port city seemed like just the place to do it. Besides, Daphene had always dreamed of living a good deal of time someplace where she could walk along the beach. I also loved it that the Jaguars were owned by a Rugged Billionaire whom I had studied before. As mentioned earlier, Shahid Khan had built a billion-dollar net worth in two businesses with the second being the Jaguars. In 2017 we began the search for a good location to house our national training center, and at the same time we planned a company-wide convention for BoxDrop™ at the Hyatt in downtown Jacksonville on the St. Johns River. As we got to know the economic development people and the convention community, we told them our long-term plans in the Jacksonville area and expressed an interest in being part of the city's further development. Before we knew it, Shahid Khan and his wife, Ann, invited us to join them in their owner's suite during a Jaguars versus the Cincinnati Bengals home football game.

What a day and football game that was! We were able to fly my father down to Florida to be with us, and we also included our then-twenty-four-year-old son, Aaron, who was working in the company's BoxDrop™ expansion team out of the Jacksonville national training center. He had opened and helped us sell two corporate BoxDrop™ Mattress locations as well and was now helping us with recruiting. Game day started with an on-field access pass that provided a closer look at the team warm-ups from the sidelines, along with introductions to some of the Jaguar cheerleaders and special NFL veteran players who are part of the NFL Legends program. It was a beautiful day, and everyone was all smiles as the players ran right past us, giving us high fives as they came out onto the field for their warm-up. We were able to take pictures with the cheerleaders and various NFL veterans too. That was also the first time we met Donvovin Darius, who played nine years for the Jaguars and was an all-pro safety. He represented the team as one of their All-Pro Legends and was ranked as the sixteenth most influential player during their 25th year anniversary. He was also the NFL's South East Legends representative and one of the greatest safeties ever to play the game. That chance meeting led to me developing a great relationship with Donovin, who is now one of my best business friends. Once again, the rewards of being a Rugged often exceed the costs.

Meeting Donovin on the field and discussing a possible speaking engagement for him at our upcoming national conference might never have happened had we not intentionally decided to seek ways to connect our football entertainment passion with our business passion. Donovin's energy and eye-piercing contact at that moment, even though he couldn't know we were looking for a possible speaker, were impressive. He has such a professional and captivating presence. How far has that meeting taken us? Well, Donovin spoke at the conference and naturally was a big hit, which led to his becoming a permanent part of Retail Service Systems' training team. It also led to him becoming a part of our Rugged Entrepreneur venture offering training, consulting, and apparel. (Check out Rugged Entrepreneur.com.)

In less than three years, Donovin has become part of four different businesses we have. The crown jewel of that day, of course, was spending so much unique time with Mr. Khan, a true Rugged Multibillionaire, and having my wife, father, and son there with me. Mr. Khan and his wife, Ann, were incredible hosts. They were passionate about the team and game and were engaged the whole time. When my wife and I thanked Mrs. Khan for the invitation, she treated us as if she had known us for years. The Khans met in college and you can tell that they love what they are doing together, combining their entertainment, football, and business passions.

The day ended with the Jaguars beating the Bengals 23–7 and with all of us hoarse from cheering so wildly. We now have six very special pub table seats for Jaguars games on the forty-five-yard line. When we fly very serious and successful Rugged Entrepreneur customers into our national training center for some special Donovin Darius "Next Level Training," we also love to host them at a Jaguars game. The entertaining sport of football has become such an integral part of our training and work with Rugged Entrepreneurs in some of our businesses, I have memorabilia in my office that reflects our ongoing experiences with the Jaguars, Shahid Khan, and Donovin Darius. One of those pieces is a 2012 autographed issue of *Forbes* magazine with Mr. Khan on the cover after he had just bought the Jaguars in January of that year. Another is my helmet and football autographed by Donovin Darius. But a picture of my father and son standing and talking with self-made Rugged Billionaire Shahid Khan is truly a priceless treasure to me because it recalls a day when three generations of Andrew entrepreneurs—two of whom have already become self-made Rugged Millionaires—all got to stretch, see, and think about what could be as they got to know a Rugged Billionaire.

Again, I am telling you all of this to illustrate the huge potential that joining your entertainment passion with your business passion represents. As I pointed out, my study of the differences between self-made Rugged Millionaires and Billionaires indicates two significant distinctions. One of those is their level of skill development and the other involves turning their entertainment interests into business interests. This amazing pairing seems to have developed the mental toughness of many Rugged Billionaires as well as their fortunes. Having learned that and knowing that Daff and I both love football almost as much as we love building businesses, we decided to intentionally work toward bringing those two passions together. In the process, we've also learned that once Ruggeds intentionally envision something, they figure out a way to make that vision a reality. Often, that reality is far better than what you imagined when you first started envisioning it. That was certainly the case for us.

Now empowering former professional and college athletes as Rugged Entrepreneurs has become a bigger part of our business and life than it ever could have been had we just remained content to be fans. From Next Level All-Pro Training to our Rugged Entrepreneur development programs, we have tied the NFL and other sport stars to multiple companies, touching many entrepreneurs' lives and businesses. You don't necessarily have to see all the future details of something before you start taking action. In fact, it's sometimes impossible to anticipate all those details. You just need to be mentally tough enough to think big and expect something great.

Donovin Darius was one of the first key people to help us connect championship athletes with the Ruggeds we inspire and train. He was also highly involved with us building our national training center and events around TIIA Bank Field, which is the home of the Jaguars and where we've held many events. His work with us continues to set a terrific precedent for what we're doing with the many other athletes who have joined us, and as we expand into other sports besides our beloved football.

While my wife was no great fan of either boxing or mixed martial arts when we started this adventure, she knew I boxed in college and that I love the sport and all its new derivatives. Given that passion, she understood when I pursued an athlete from that world to participate in our work. In 2018, with the help of one of my favorite Ruggeds, Steve Silver, who has generated hundreds of millions of dollars through multiple businesses he created, we connected with Henry Cejudo. Henry was, at one time, the youngest U.S. Olympic gold medal holder and still is the youngest to receive the gold in freestyle wrestling. After telling Henry about what we do, Steve Silver was able to interest him in coming to speak to about 400 Ruggeds at an event we were holding in Texas. The impact this then-reigning UFC Flyweight World Champion made upon our group of Ruggeds was extraordinary. Winners have similar habits and stories, but few are more Rugged than Henry's. He was one of seven children born to Mexican immigrant parents, and despite moving nearly fifty times throughout his childhood, he became a four-time state champion with a record of one hundred and fifty wins and zero defeats in high school before becoming a resident athlete at the U.S. Olympic Training Center.

Not long after Henry spoke at our Rugged event, I sat in an arena in Chicago, Illinois, with Daff, Steve Silver, and one of Steve's sons, Troy, and watched as Henry won a second UFC world title belt in a decision against the bantamweight holder, Marlon Moraes. In winning that second belt that night, Henry became one of very few champions to hold two UFC world title belts simultaneously, and we were there live with business partners to see it happen and share in that great moment.

Since we began following the lead of the Rugged Billionaires we admire by combining our passion for sports entertainment with our passion for business, we realize that doing this is way more entertaining than just being a consumer of entertainment itself. The business results also extended far beyond the value of us being entertained. Today, we are thrilled to entertain others this way, thrilled to raise our mental toughness quotient this way, and thrilled to connect multiple champion athletes and sports organizations with multiple entrepreneurs and businesses, all while building our own organizations.

"M" Is for Meditating: The last two components in this mental-strengthening exercise are the most challenging to do and also take the most dedicated time to perfect, but I will tell you from personal experience, they are extremely important. When I was a younger entrepreneur, I was not humble enough to have a Rugged Intellect nor did I understand how to get to the state where I could tap into the universal wisdom around me. In fact, meditating was not something I felt a need for, nor was it something I wanted to learn to do. I am not a meditation expert now, either, so this will be something you will have to work on and figure out for yourself. For me, it is not a yoga thing or a sit in some odd position burning incense while you hum or repeat some silent mantra kind of thing. Rather, it is about slowing things down and getting in a mindset where I see how small I am in this great world and at the same time feel empowered in a way that makes me thankful for all the opportunities I have to do something in this life. That is how I create the path that opens the doorway to universal wisdom, which I can then tap into. It's up to you to discover ways to get yourself in that same awesome place.

I have now learned through practice that at least two things can get me there. One is spent during the early morning in a place where I can see God's incredible sunrise. Its power and awe—especially when viewed over an ocean, a lake, or in the mountains—are humbling. As I have explained, the early morning is also when your mind is the clearest because it's rested. There are no distractions before everyone else wakes up. When I see that sunrise, my mind just slows down in thanks and wonder at the world's power and beauty. Everything I am working on mentally just seems to fold into an order and an intentional design. I can see how things and people work and fit together as if they are puzzle pieces falling into place. I can think through my actions as if they are advanced moves in a multi-dimensional chess game. It is a mental state where I am able to tap into universal wisdom and let it help me creatively see how things might play out in different scenarios. I can imagine potential outcomes down the road and better assess the risks associated with those results. There is a mathematical quality about the "if this, then that" nature of the process.

The second thing for me is taking a long walk with my wife, either in the mountains, around a lake with a rugged and beautiful view, or on a beach with the sound of breaking waves. Something about water has always helped me get into deep thought. I'm not sure if it is the fact that there is so much I don't know about its depth, volume, what lies beneath the surface, the difference in sound above and below, the power of the pressure at certain depths, or its force against the environment. Being with Daff doesn't prevent me from getting into that mindspace because I am so at peace with her. I trust and respect her so much that when we walk together, my mind slips into that place naturally, and I am able to share with her everything that I see about the moves on the chessboard. It doesn't happen during every walk, but it continues to be something that occurs more and more over time.

Those walks with Daff are a sure advantage for me, as I truly know that most couples do not share the deep business connection we do and shouldn't be expected or forced to. It has to come naturally for a couple, and it has to be what they both want. For us, that connection happened almost by accident when she began helping me with my rodeo production company, then the beverage wholesale business, and soon everything else. Daff was and still is my biggest cheerleader and I am hers. I will not call it "the only sure advantage," because it is not. It is just something I wouldn't want to miss sharing with people in case they might be able to duplicate and benefit from that kind of close support too.

I believe there are numerous ways to get yourself to a mental place where you are meditating and accessing the universal wisdom of the world around you. You have to approach it with the same discipline and determination as you approach exercise. The more you work at it, the easier it is to tap into it and stay there. I have read that some people combine it with their daily exercise. They say that they can ease into the mind frame best when they are taking a morning run, bike ride, or when they are rowing. It occurs when it is just you and the exercise, not necessarily when you are in a class or group setting. I have also read about people who have accessed universal wisdom when reading and thinking about their spirituality. It is a practice within many religions. As I've said before, I came to it my own way and know that you will too. Just remember that after emerging from your meditation, you must work at using whatever insight you find there. Following up on your ideas is much more powerful than just thinking about them.

"E" Is for Educating: In the same way that you must find your path into meditation to improve your mental toughness quotient, you have to figure out a personal way for you to become an educator of others. There are multiple approaches. Some of these approaches require finding an audience and others do not. As an entrepreneur reading this book, you likely have employees, customers, vendors, or any combination of the three. In your personal life, you have family and friends and you may even belong to some kind of social group, such as a house of worship or a civic organization. With access to individuals and groups such as these, there are many opportunities to communicate with others on a topic you are passionate about. One way to get the courage to educate is to simply substitute the word "educate" in your mind with the word "share." Initially, you start teaching or educating by sharing thoughts on a special interest or hobby. This practice of sharing will help you speak comfortably, anticipate others' questions, and clarify your thoughts so you communicate even better the next time. Ultimately, you will be ready to share what you know with larger groups. Creating teaching opportunities for yourself is a great way to further develop mental toughness. It forces you out of your comfort zone and stretches you to think about how your knowledge can potentially multiply good work. It also expands communities and creates networks.

If you have had any experience in sales, you have likely already engaged in this process, as all sales pitches require some teaching. An assertive sales pitch will educate the potential buyer as to why the product or service being represented adds a value benefit to their life or business. A lot of people are afraid to enter a direct selling field and that is too bad for them, as it is one of the best ways to begin developing excellent communication and teaching skills. All Ruggeds must possess these qualities.

You may be thinking, *What topic do I have to communicate or share?* Earlier in this book I told you how my passion for learning about capitalism, free enterprise, and entrepreneurialism grew by reading various books such as *How Capitalism Saved America* by Thomas DiLorenzo and *How Capitalism Will Save Us* by Steve Forbes. These two books made me see how little I learned about true American history in high school and college. There is so much more to our history than the dates of various events or key battles and wars. Realizing that I had been deprived of a deeper education, particularly about our ingenious system of economics, I had a burning desire to learn more. That desire was compounded by the discovery of just how entrepreneurial our forefathers were. My pursuit sparked an impulse to share the historical information I was learning whenever a good opportunity arose, whether it was in passing conversation or in deeper talks. I was amazed at how easy it was to find places in a normal conversation where I could point out facts and theories linking history with modern-day life. I used the stories that I learned about our past to complement something a person was saying or doing. Connecting history to what someone was telling me in a current conversation often attraccted people's attention and interested them in hearing more about how their words or actions prompted me to think about that historic reference or example. That led to even deeper conversations wherein I found myself telling stories and literally giving mini history lessons. After learning how capitalism actually saved America and about how entrepreneurialism is the heartbeat of this nation, I was fascinated. My personal study was a great exercise that increased my mental toughness at the same time as it increased my pride in being an entrepreneur myself. As someone embracing the personal independence of making it on my own, I was connecting to the Rugged roots of our ancestors who also took pride in their independence as they sought to make it as pioneers in a new land.

If you want to know more about people like this, exploring the life of George Washington is a great place to start. Everyone knows him as a soldier commissioned to be the general of the American revolutionary army to fight the British for our independence, and ultimately as a founding father of our great nation and the first president of the United States. But did you know that he was also a very successful entrepreneur who founded and developed many businesses before and after the revolution? While wealth was not measured in those days as it is today, some say Washington was the wealthiest man of his time.

Washington's father died when he was just eleven years old, so he had to grow up fast. At an early age, he learned surveying and loved being outdoors, riding horses, and exploring the terrain around him. In 1750, when he was just seventeen, Washington was appointed by Culpeper county to be the county surveyor. Can you imagine a seventeen-year-old in today's world being appointed as the county surveyor for a major county? When he was nineteen, Washington's uncle and aunt died and left him their estate, which he had already helped them survey and build. The very next year, due to his surveying skills and horsemanship, the Royal Governor of Virginia (the colonies were still under British rule at the time) appointed Washington as a major in the Virginia militia to fight in the French and Indian War. His leadership in that event led to his appointment as the Commander and Chief of all the British forces assigned to defend the Virginia frontier. During these early years of military leadership, Washington was also building Mount Vernon. His broad-minded thinking as a young military strategist and land surveyor propelled him to become a Rugged Entrepreneur in multiple industries.

Having read excerpts from several of Washington's letters, memoirs, and journals, I believe that he somehow learned to tap into what we have spoken about as Rugged Intellect. He was a proud but humble man with a disciplined Christian faith and a deep sense of gratitude. He kept prayer journals and regularly appealed to God for insight. I consider this his form of meditation—his own personalized means of tapping into universal wisdom. Because Washington was diligent about reflecting on life and writing daily, he has been broadly studied and written about by historians. I learned much of this through reading books about him, but today you can easily access this information on the Internet. If you do explore Washington's past, I'm sure you will see how his business wisdom informed everything he did. It enabled him to see the value in and prospect of creating the kind of society in which we live now.

Over time, he created a vast tobacco business, built mills to cut logs into timber for construction, and established a shipbuilding business that made schooners for fishing. When profits from tobacco shrank, he switched to growing grains and hemp, whose values had risen. Next, he built gristmills for grinding and storing those grains. Using the grains and further extending his product base, Washington built a distilling business that grew from one to five stills and profitably produced and sold thousands of gallons of whiskey annually as one of the largest distillers in the nation. Our forefathers, both men and women, had to be Rugged to survive and, especially, to thrive. Many of them developed a broad array of interest and skills, making them Renaissance people, much like Washington.

Washington was so diligent that before he died, he penned his own twenty-page will. It was the second he had written, and it was extremely detailed. You can and should go find a copy of it online to read for yourself as it is a public document. There you will see how he doled out each of his assets and specifically advised his beneficiaries on how to care for their inheritance. Today, drawing up the paperwork to leave an estate with thousands of acres and numerous businesses would require an estate planner and an expert tax attorney. Talk about educating yourself and others!

During those pioneering years in America's history, we had the highest percentage of entrepreneurs per capita than any other time. Familiarizing yourself with our forefathers and their broader entrepreneurial backgrounds, achievements, and spirit should inspire the pioneer in you. Learning about the protections they implemented to preserve entrepreneurialism, such as ownership rights, common law, free enterprise, low taxation, and no taxation without representation, should encourage you to take advantage of the foundation they provided and motivate you to build something enterprising of your own on top of it.

It is difficult for me to explain how much learning about American entrepreneurial history raised my healthy pride. It is empowering to know that I am connected to the Rugged Entrepreneurial spirit of George Washington just by being a citizen of this great nation. I am in no way related to George Washington by blood, but as Americans we all share a deep connection with our historic ancestors as much as we do with our genetic ancestors. I encourage you to embrace the best parts of that Rugged heritage and allow them to inspire you. I have historic pictures of Washington and several antique history textbooks about him from the early 1800s in my office as part of my commitment to "surround" myself with inspiration. Today's media, politicians, and some schoolteachers and professors tend to look away from the positives and focus only on the painful, obviously negative, and complex issues of slavery when they discuss this period in our history and people such as Washington. They are not wrong to do so; to be great we must always look at the rights and wrongs in life and in cultures to make things better, more just, and equal in opportunity for all in the present and future.

In looking at how Washington saw and executed the finality of his life, he ultimately had grave misgivings about slavery, and upon reflection made a final and important statement on the subject through his actions. If you read his last will and testament, as I suggested, you will see that he ordered the slaves on his properties to be freed and also made provisions for their education. We talked earlier about learning from our failings and this is certainly an example of that. It in no way made up for the wrongs of slavery, and while this book is not about addressing those wrongs—it's about Rugged Entrepreneurialism and its movement through history—it felt important to acknowledge. When we look at the whole of Washington's journey, we cannot gloss over the negative parts of it, but it is also important to find the good side of what he and some of the other Rugged Entrepreneurs of historic times from all cultures and races accomplished. His examples of entrepreneurialism, his enterprise building, his ability to see the interconnectedness of businesses, and his nimbleness amidst changing market conditions are examples of Rugged Entrepreneurialism in that time and can be an example to help you cultivate mental toughness for yourself as a Rugged Entrepreneur who must make decisions and navigate times as they exist today.

If you're concerned that you don't have enough knowledge on a topic to draw an audience, then start without one. Pick a topic directly connected to your business. Maybe you can explore your industry's history, or you can focus on how your business can solve current problems. If you have to, do as I did and study the history of entrepreneurialism in America. From one of those beginnings, keep a journal the way George Washington did. Record your experiences and thoughts. In time you will realize that you have a larger body of knowledge than you thought you did, and certainly you will have a larger body of knowledge than when you started. Think of this practice as laying the foundation for writing your own book someday because your perspective and experiences can help shape and promote Rugged Entrepreneurialism too. This is almost exactly how the adventure of writing this book began for me. If I can do it, I am sure you can too. As you build your knowledge and passion on the topic of your choice, it will automatically work its way into conversations, and you will soon find yourself engaging others in teaching moments.

If you are still not sure that educating others is an important aspect of being successful, think about all the great coaches that are out there in the world of sports. All of the coaches I have ever studied understand and expressly *teach* mental toughness because they know it's the gateway to achieving goals.

As you've read earlier, we loved having the Clemson Tigers' Zac Brooks as an intern at my wife's research and development BoxDrop™ test location. While we were creating that program with Zac on our team, we also got the opportunity to see inside Zac's other team. We met coaches, toured facilities, and studied one of the greatest football coaches of our time, Dabo Swinney. Coach Swinney was a former receiver at the University of Alabama, who at one time had his mother come live with him on campus because she was homeless. I mention that here because it's a great Rugged story, a true mark of his character, and no doubt a hardship that made him mentally tougher. As a coach, Dabo Swinney is an innate teacher. In an article about the great Clemson–Georgia rivalry, he talked about how the prospect of playing Georgia annually is a good thing if both teams can make it happen, as they did for many years. In that same article he admitted, "When I got the job, I didn't think we knew how to win—we didn't have the mindset, and the mentality, and mental toughness it takes." That's why Coach Swinney was so aggressive about scheduling and playing great teams who weren't in his conference, including Georgia. He even nicknamed one of those games the "SHO'NUFF" game. Swinney is known for his immense passion and for educating his team in his own unique way. Lining up games with tough opponents outside of the normal schedule provides an important lesson about practice and raising the stakes by seeking out worthy opponents. He recruits aggressively, coaches aggressively, and expects great results. Mental toughness is one of the pillars upon which he builds his championship players, teams, and organizations. He incorporates it into the Clemson program intentionally. You can learn a lot about how to build mental toughness in yourself, your people, and your organization(s) through Coach Swinney's wise example.

Once you develop a comfort with educating others, it becomes part of your customized skill set. Learning how to educate yourself and others should be ingrained into the training and development programs of every organization. It is so important to me that I intentionally develop teaching skills within the people who work in our various organizations. Such education prepares them for greater responsibilities and leadership roles as the organization grows. Teach your leaders how to become good speakers and by that, I mean teach them to be able to speak from the heart rather than from notes. Teach them how to conduct and run different types of unifying meetings. Teach them how to identify opportunities for team building and delegation. These are some of the educational foundations I believe most organizations should build into their DNA, though many do not as they know very little or nothing about them.

Like all of the other components of this R.A.I.S.E.M.E. program, educating others can have an exponentially positive effect on the growth of your business. The practice of teaching others increases the mental toughness quotient of the organization itself, not just you as its leader. All organizations have their own MTQ, and its leaders need to be experts on how to personally build and enhance it. Teaching yields competitive, mentally strong people and teams that are customer-driven and expect to be better than the competition. Companies that create such an atmosphere often experience disruptive breakthroughs and/or dynamic growth patterns.

Now that you have the tools for creating your own R.A.I.S.E.M.E. program, go make it a reality. Continuously work on your mental toughness because the business world is fierce and full of challenges. You will naturally anticipate some of those challenges, but some will be completely unexpected. Dealing with the unexpected ones requires a lot of fortitude. If you are not mentally tough enough to handle them, you will fold. You don't want to find yourself in a situation where you are unable to make crucial decisions with enough speed and confidence to beat the competition or be on top of a crisis that destroys businesses that lack mentally tough leadership.

Our MTQ and our business teams' MTQ have developed to levels high enough to help steer them through unexpected calamities including the depression relating to the COVID-19 crisis of 2020. In that tumultuous business time, our businesses under two large umbrella companies adapted and grew. I credit much of that not only to Daphene's and my MTQ but also to the elevated MTQ of our teams and customers. Looking specifically at BoxDrop during that time, when most brick-and-mortar-centric businesses in the home furnishing industry were devastated and suffered dramatic losses, BoxDrop thrived as a national chain. It was BoxDrop's organizational MTQ that empowered the management team to pivot and take a strong business position, which then influenced and guided the national chain to follow suit. That organizational mental toughness is the singular most important reason that the BoxDrop™ Rugged Nation grew double digits through those chaotic times when competitors with weak MTQs were wrought with confusion, calamity, and indecisiveness. Mental toughness will get you through the inevitable challenges that occur in an ever-changing environment, and a strong MTQ will empower your organizations to be disruptive.

I speak from experience as illustrated here and by the fact that Daff and I have survived dramatic life-altering ups and downs. We've gone from being millionaires to having almost nothing twice in our evolution as Ruggeds. During one of those times, we fell from a comfortable multi-six-figure income to a place where we were scratching dirt just to keep two small businesses alive on roughly $6,000 a month. We had to sell a 6,700-square-foot home that we owned and move into a 1,500-square-foot rental while Daff went back to work full time and I took on two part-time jobs. Ruggeds do what it takes to rise back up and are mentally tough enough to handle it. The second time, we made the very tough choice to engage in two nearly simultaneous legal battles involving different businesses we owned. One of those businesses was paying us a large residual-based income, but we came to believe there were some hypocrisies we could not be part of. The only conscionable thing to do in that case was to object and take our investment elsewhere, even though it meant leaving already-earned income on the table. The other battle was very serious and involved threats against us. The stand we took in that situation also required us to make decisions that substantially reduced our income and impacted our family and lifestyle. Once again, we were forced to sell a home and downsize.

Are you mentally tough enough to walk away from financial security and start all over again to preserve your principles? I am not saying you will have to, but if you must, can you?

If you are bullied by attorneys, customers, creditors, or the press because your situation has drawn either good or bad attention, will you have the mental stamina to stand your ground? Can you deal with the prospect of people lying about you to serve their own interests? Will you address their lies to prove them wrong? When the naysayers are banging at your door telling you that you cannot withstand the fight, will you be strong enough to move ahead anyway and prevail?

I refer to the poems "Desiderata" by Max Ehrmann and "If" by Rudyard Kipling several times in this book because both have proved to be guiding words in difficult times. "Desiderata" helps me navigate storms calmly, and "If" encourages me to stay in the fight with dignity. I've burned the first verse of "If" in my mind and offer it here for you to do the same:

> *"If you can keep your head when all about you*
> *Are losing theirs and blaming it on you,*
> *If you can trust yourself when all men doubt you,*
> *But make allowance for their doubting too;*
> *If you can wait and not be tired by waiting,*
> *Or being lied about, don't deal in lies,*
> *Or being hated, don't give way to hating,*
> *And yet don't look too good, nor talk too wise:*

The challenge with naysayers is that there is always one within earshot whispering things to try to get you to make bad decisions, waste time with other negative influences, or promise things you cannot deliver to a customer, employee, or investor. As he or she drones on, you can barely hear your own thoughts. You must be mentally tough enough to tune out the naysayer. Being mentally resilient means staying with people in challenging times and also walking away from a deal, customer, employee, vendor, or even a business partner if those are the right things to do. If you want to be a Rugged, you have to have the fortitude to make the right choices no matter how difficult they may be and no matter how many others may disagree. The bigger your organization gets, the more mental toughness you need to guide it wisely.

Companies often reach a point of success and then flatten out because there is either a lack of vision or a lack of mental toughness. Both are necessary to make the decisions that set a company in new directions or empower it to be a disruptor.

There is another important reason why mental toughness counts. In a growing organization, choosing leaders from a group of many who all believe they are qualified often creates a level of disappointment, envy, and even anger amongst those who are too competitive or too egocentric. If a leader is not mentally tough enough, some of these problematic individuals will overrun them. A leader without the right MTQ will ignore those individuals, whereas one with *fortitudo mentis* teaches them to focus on creating their own opportunities instead of wishing for someone else's. A mentally tough leader is willing to communicate directly with these individuals and teach them the principle benefits of an organization committed to creating opportunity. Mentally tough leaders possess Rugged Intellect. They know or quickly identify which problems merit attention and which don't, and they are always willing to deal with the important ones head on. They concentrate on fostering unity and on rooting out those who continuously cause conflict without a reason for constructive benefit.

If leaders lack this mental toughness, they will make poor decisions. The need for more mental toughness in less developed leaders is particularly evident when they try to make decisions based on some sort of "fairness quotient." In today's overhyped mess of political correctness, negative influences are emboldened to whisper things to weaken your resolve based on what the world seems to be saying on any topic at any given moment. Pay increases, for instance, don't need to be given out equally to everyone; they should be given in accordance with performance. Every team or player on every team doesn't win a trophy or MVP award in sports, and they don't in business either. Similarly, successful corporations shouldn't be shamed for their success. Negative influences will use political correctness to make you question your decisions, as it's an effective tool to distract you. They have no real desire to see you succeed. The world loves and hates successful entrepreneurs all at the same time. Only a small percentage of people (10 to 15 percent) choose to become entrepreneurs and a large percentage of the world's millionaires and billionaires (70 to 80 percent) come from that group. These highly successful entrepreneurs have little to no interest in making the 80 to 90 percent of people who are not entrepreneurs look bad. Doing that is not part of their business plan. Even so, many people who have never waded into the waters of entrepreneurialism or have no idea what it takes to be a Rugged, see the success of others as a something that reflects poorly on them. In their minds, our success is like a mirror that casts a negative image of them as bad, lazy, or unsuccessful by comparison. They can often become jealous and, in an attempt to avoid what they perceive as being seen in an unflattering light, say and do things to try to break the mirror, or at least mask the impression they think it makes. It is a dynamic that has always existed between Ruggeds and others. It appears that a large percentage of the world will always speak negatively about capitalism, free enterprise, entrepreneurialism, and those who have attained success because of their work in it. You have to grow your mental toughness in order to handle that negativity, as some of it will come from people very close to you, including family members and friends.

In our businesses that empower entrepreneurs who own unique retail or service business models, we teach those entrepreneurs how to be mentally strong enough to handle naysayers of all types. We teach them that naysayers range from industry experts to well-intentioned acquaintances, friends, or loved ones they respect. We teach them how to avoid being sidetracked by bad or unsolicited advice in person, through advertising, and through the media. The world is full of armchair experts who are strongly opinionated without evidence of success in your field of endeavor. We use a story to help ingrain this message in their minds so they are able to deal with such advisors, critics, and other detractors. I share this story with you now.

The Man Who Sold Hot Dogs

There was once a man who lived by the side of a highway. He built a stand to make and sell delicious hot dogs. He was hard of hearing, so he had no radio. He had poor vision, too, so he didn't read the newspaper, watch TV, search the Internet, or engage in using social media. He was very cut off from outside influences. He did, however, prepare and sell very tasty hot dogs. He posted signs along the highway telling everyone how good they were, then stood at the curb and cried out to all who passed his way, "Stop and buy a hot dog—they're the best in town."

The people who bought his hot dogs loved them and always came back for more, so he increased his meat and bun orders and bought a bigger stove to take care of all the extra business. He posted more signs and continued to see his customer base grow. With business now booming, he asked his son to come and help him.

But then something dramatic happened. His son, who had been well educated, said, "Father, haven't you been reading the news, listening to the radio, watching TV, or checking the Internet? There's a big recession about to hit. The current climate is terrible. There's political unrest, immigration problems, racial tensions, pay disparities, rising living costs, strikes, pollution, global warming, corruption, discord between minorities and majorities, the rich and poor, the capitalists and socialists." Whereupon his father thought, *My son's been well educated. He reads the papers, listens to the radio, watches TV, and uses the Internet, so he must know what's best.*

Without wasting another minute, the father cut his meat and bun orders, took down all of his billboards, and no longer bothered to stand by the side of the road promoting his tasty hot dogs. Sales plummeted almost overnight to a fraction of what they used to be.

Soon the father said to the son: **"You're right, son. This is a terrible recession we are getting hit by."**

—Author Unknown

I am sure you see the point in my telling this story here. It is an example of why an entrepreneur must be mentally tough enough to avoid bad advice, even if it comes from someone you love or hold in high regard. To be a Rugged Entrepreneur, you have to develop and continue to increase your MTQ because the situations and decisions you will face grow more challenging as your organization succeeds and grows. You have very likely been using some of the qualities I address in this book without giving a name to them and without intentionally working on developing them. Many people, for instance, exercise a fervent work ethic before they ever realize that is what it could be called or that it is something to be nurtured. The same is true with mental toughness. I was already displaying and relying on it before I recognized its existence or importance. Being mentally tough enough to disregard bad advice or to stay away from associations that are not productive may be intuitive at first, but it is not always as easy as you think. *Do you have the mental toughness to make your own choices? How about the mental fortitude to avoid being strong-armed by what I will call "workplace hostage takers"?*

The first time I realized that mental toughness needed to be consciously developed the way one develops a muscle was when I had finally become an owner in a business with more than fifty employees. It was during my years in the beverage wholesale business. Every Monday morning at 5:00 a.m., we met with our pre-sales-people and merchandisers (the guys who drove the trucks and delivered product). On one particular Monday morning at about 4:45, just before the meeting was about to begin, the merchandiser-trainer came to my office and asked to have a word. I replied, "Certainly, come on in." He sat down and said, "Scott, you have a decision to make before the sales meeting." Then he proceeded to tell me that he and the other merchandisers had been discussing pay increases and that unless we gave them all an eight-cent raise for every case delivered, they were collectively walking that morning.

What a way to start the day. I thought about it for a few moments and for some reason the only thought that came to my mind was that this son of a gun was trying to hold me hostage. He was using timing to his advantage. If we couldn't make all of the deliveries without him and the current group of merchandisers we'd be in a difficult position. I knew instantly that if I allowed him to give me an ultimatum that way, he could do it over and over again. That was easy enough to surmise, but I still had a very disturbing and immediate situation to deal with, which was the real possibility that they would, in fact, all walk and we'd miss making all of our deliveries over next two to three days. A walkout like that could set us back a week or more. Fortunately for me, he had come alone to represent the group. Because the sales meeting was imminent, I didn't have any way to say, "Time out, let me think about this." A decision had to be made right then and there. The easy and also mentally weak decision would have been to simply agree to the raise.

Instead, I told this merchandiser-trainer to sit down, and I proceeded to compliment him on being the type of leader and communicator that I had known him to be. I didn't get angry, but I told him that his decision to approach me this way was a very serious one. I asked him why the merchandisers felt like a raise was merited. I also asked if he thought making a demand like this on such short notice would actually force me to say yes. He explained that he knew merchandisers who worked for other beverage wholesalers and he gathered from speaking with them that he and his merchandisers were being paid more than two of those and less than two of the others. He said that he and the merchandiser team believed they should at least be paid an amount equal to the average of the higher two. He told me that they had all agreed over the weekend that the best way to draw attention to their importance was to make the demand before the sales meeting. Asking this merchandiser-trainer to explain how it all came together gave me some time to think while I listened to him. A Rugged's mental toughness is crucial in those times when there isn't a lot of time to think through your decision. This was one of those times. I told him that he was one of our best people and that I would hate to lose him. I then stood up and suggested that we literally switch chairs for a moment. Once that was done, I explained to him that there were six beverage wholesale businesses covering the region and that five other people sat in chairs like the one he was sitting in now. I also told him that I was on the state's wholesalers board and that I worked with all of the other leaders to determine the better business practices for the industry. I then told him that I typically spoke with the other five once or twice a month and that CDL (Commercial Drivers Licensed) drivers presented one of our industry's biggest challenges. I asked him if he knew any of those other five leaders. He said that he had never met any of them but that he did know the name of at least one. I then said, "Answer me one question: How well do you think any of those other wholesalers would take it if their merchandising leader tried to hold them hostage in a situation like this?" This merchandiser-trainer admitted that they probably wouldn't like it.

I then went on to explain to him that he had two choices and he should consider them both from his position in the chair he was presently sitting in (my chair), thinking like me, or like any of those other general managers. His first option was to gather his merchandisers in the conference room, remind them that they all had a choice about where they worked, and to tell them that he was choosing to stay because I was willing to work with him on identifying ways to help merchandisers increase their sales opportunities, particularly ways to gain display space in grocery and convenient stores. As a part of that option, he could also tell them that we would create a merchandisers advisory group made up of him and two other merchandisers elected by the whole team. He could also tell them that I would meet with that group once a month to implement merchandiser programs to help generate even more opportunities for them. I explained that we were willing to add some incentive pay, but he had to design and implement a program that would allow us to measure and grade the work the merchandisers were doing so performance incentives rewarded those who actually earned them.

I then told this merchandiser-trainer that option number two was for them all to walk out as threatened. But I also told him that if they did, our sales manager was going to round up our six supervisors and each of them, along with me, would take a route that day to make deliveries ourselves. I added that it would take us a week or two to catch up, but we were determined to survive intact. I also told him that we would hire new merchandisers and that before I left to drive one of the routes myself that morning, I would be calling all of those other general managers to let them know what transpired. A list of the names of those who walked out would be faxed to them and his would be on the top of that list. I told him that I would do everything in my power to explain to them that he led the uprising and that they should be very concerned about it happening in their operations if they chose to hire him. I then asked him, "If you were them and you found out about this scenario and the possibility that you would try to one day hold them hostage, too, would you hire you?"

This merchandiser-trainer thought about it for a few seconds and he looked at me and said, "You can't just keep them from hiring any of us if they want to." I then told him that he was right, I couldn't make them do that, but I could make sure all of the other GMs knew that he was the ringleader and that if they hired him, they might have to deal with the same turmoil and strong-arm tactics he was using on me. I then stood up and said "I have a lot to organize; if you're going to lead this walk out, let's get to it. Do you want to call everyone together and vote on identifying the two other merchandisers who will be working with you on a merchandiser advisory board? Or do you want your face to appear on a poster at beverage wholesalers throughout the region as a most-wanted hostage taker?"

I didn't know how he would respond; I just knew that I couldn't allow myself to be "held at gunpoint" that way, figuratively speaking. I couldn't give in to what was being demanded, but I also couldn't just fire everybody. He looked at me and asked, "How do I explain to the group that we are going to set up an advisory board?" On the inside I was breathing a sigh of relief. I knew that he didn't want to lead a walk out. I said, "It's easy. Just round everyone up in the conference room and I will explain our conversation and your lead role in making improvements for them and for the company. I will tell them that we are going to vote on the two others and that the three of you would be meeting with me over the next few weeks to create a new program." He quickly asked if we could also implement a program that allowed merchandisers to wear shorts in the summer months. I agreed and said, "Let's tell the group that this will be the first initiative you will implement, effective immediately, and that there would be other initiatives to follow." Suddenly, this merchandiser-trainer saw that he had gotten a win and that I was going to empower him in his leadership role. He went from antagonist hostage taker to team player in an instant.

I am happy to say, we didn't lose any merchandisers that day. Even so, it was something that really took me back and made me think deeply. I thanked God for the wisdom that rose up in me that morning. Of course, the event remained on my mind for quite a while after that.

That was the day I realized mental toughness was a quality with a name and that, as an entrepreneur, I had to work on strengthening it. In an odd way I am grateful for this man's attempt to corner me. I now teach other leaders how to do their best to avoid it ever happening to them and to be ready for it if and when it does. You have to be thankful for the things that make you Rugged. That said, I have since developed a *huge* disdain for hostage takers and those who weaponize negotiations after work has been started. I have been in several other situations where they've operated since that first event. Hostage takers, by the way, are not always employees. They can be vendors, service providers, competitors, and even family members.

Also beware of *unprofessional* professionals who flaunt their expertise in confusing ways while charging large hourly fees. People in fields such as accounting, consulting, information technology and software, and especially those in the legal profession, come to mind. Of course, not everyone in these careers will try to take you hostage but, given their specialized knowledge, it is easy for them to do so, and for many it's an intentional aspect of their business plan.

Generalizing attorneys as a whole would not be right, as there are certainly people with good character and those with bad character in every type of group. That said, there is a reason why many studies, including those from Forbes, Pew, and Gallup, consistently rank attorneys as somewhere between the first and fifth most disliked and least trusted professionals in America. AOL money and career expert Dawn Rosenberg McKay also ranked them low in her deep dive review of most and least popular professionals. Can we say that where there is smoke— and a lot of it—there is usually fire?

You must strengthen your mental toughness because becoming a Rugged in today's ever-growing litigious world means you are likely to need an attorney and a law firm, or possibly multiple attorneys and multiple firms, at some point in your journey. Should that happen, your organizations, and maybe even you, will have to defend against a level of moral deficiency and avarice that is difficult for most people to comprehend, let alone contend with. The more success your organization(s) have, the more mental toughness you and your teams must tirelessly develop. Success draws a swarm of greedy characters to it. It makes you a target. Directly or indirectly your detractors will engage lawyers against you. And as it happens, there are plenty of morally bankrupt attorneys who are eager to empower your detractor's lies against you and your organization(s).

Sometimes these scurrilous attorneys are the very same ones you or your organizations choose to hire and to whom you pay thousands, tens of thousands, or even hundreds of thousands of dollars. Believe me when I tell you, it takes a lot of mental toughness to handle the daily duties of being the CEO of a rapidly growing company when the very close professionals you once trusted become unethical to the point of attempting to steal from you. We have prevailed in cases of trade-secret theft and breach of contract, all the way up to fraud where I have seen a perpetrator sent to jail. Our organizations have protected intellectual property and brands nationwide, applied to patent products, and enforced protections for our customers. Others have threatened to sue us for owning domain names for certain brands, which we've either defended our right to have or restructured and successfully converted to highly profitable sales. The crafty ways greedy attorneys empower nefarious individuals or decide themselves to come after your organizations and your success is endless, and I only see it getting worse.

Let me share with you now an imaginative story about a battle between a farmer and some questionable lawyers to help demonstrate why a heightened level of mental toughness in a Rugged's world is important.

A Cautionary Tale

Rugged farmer and his beautiful wife have a small but lovely farm. When Rugged sustains a life-threatening injury, he has to take time off from working the land. Next to Rugged's small farm is a much bigger farm owned by Crooked farmer. While Rugged recuperates, Crooked and his farmhands attempt to steal some of Rugged's acreage. In the process, severe damage is done to the land. Being a frugal farmer, Rugged engages a small country lawyer and sues Crooked. Crooked, in turn, hires big city lawyers who know how to game the legal system so the case drags out in the courts for several years.

Ultimately, through hard work and truthfulness, Rugged and his country lawyer win the case. The judge orders Crooked to pay a monetary judgment to Rugged. But Crooked and his duplicitous lawyers are reluctant to pay the judgment and instead hatch a plan to extend the legal process through appeals. This allows Crooked almost two years to deplete his resources and destroy most of his farm, selling off and hiding its assets.

When Crooked finally loses all of the appeals, it is up to Rugged to collect the money that is due to him according to the judgment. But Crooked cries, "I have nothing left. My farm has been losing money for years. It is in debt and worthless." Having already spent so much time and hundreds of thousands of dollars attaining the judgment, Rugged engages new, specialized big city lawyers on a contingency fee basis to assist him in collecting the monies from Crooked. This means that the lawyers will be paid a percentage of the value of whatever they recovered on Rugged's behalf at the time they recover it. The contingency fee lawyers are confident that Crooked is lying about his financial demise and are eager to help Rugged be made whole.

The contingency fee lawyers successfully obtain a few cash payments from Crooked before the judge finally puts Crooked in jail for some of his wrongdoings. Rugged pays his lawyers the contingency fee they earned thus far from those cash payments, but the monies still owed to Rugged for damages are way larger than the collected sums.

Soon Rugged and the contingency fee lawyers discover that Crooked, enabled by his lawyers, has indeed managed to deplete everything from the Crooked farm, which was now losing money. All that is left are some old seeds, broken farm equipment, and a few outdated farming techniques that no longer work very well. Worse is the fact that these assets are subject to substantial risk because Crooked was under investigation for not paying all of the taxes on the income that the Crooked farm earned when it was successful. Crooked had also wronged several other people who might have claims against him just as Rugged did. Even without these risks, what little is left by Crooked is essentially worthless.

Rugged and his wife are further saddened to learn about the hardship that many of the honest farmhands on Crooked's farm endured while Crooked was decimating his property and tools. When it is announced that Crooked's farm is soon to be shut down, Rugged decides to explore the possibility of making something out of the assets that are left. He thinks it might help him save the farmhands who are still working on Crooked's farm and maybe one day it may make him whole for the years of work and hundreds of thousands of dollars spent while trying to repair the harm done to his own farm.

The contingency fee lawyers believe that Rugged's idea is a bad one and maintain that the Crooked Farm assets and techniques are far too broken and antiquated to ever be productive again. There is also the prospect of legal liability. Accepting the assets in lieu of the court-ordered monetary judgment could cost Rugged money, and it could also cost the contingency fee lawyers money since they are paid a percentage of the value of whatever is recovered. By their reasoning, a percentage of assets worth nothing is nothing, so they would not recover any money if Rugged pursued that path. And if they pursued that path, there is a chance that the people acquiring Crooked's assets would have to pay some of Crooked's debts. They also do not think it is wise to chance having to pay Crooked's tax bill to the IRS or any sums to Crooked's other creditors, which by now are potentially in the millions of dollars. After calling in special accountants to assess how substantial the risks might be to any future owners of the Crooked Farm assets, the attorneys tell Rugged he should not acquire the Crooked farm assets and stress that it is far too risky to consider.

Despite his contingency fee lawyers' written and verbal objections and warnings, Rugged talks to Crooked farmer and agrees to accept most of his remaining seeds, broken farm equipment, and outdated farming techniques in return for a satisfaction of the judgment that Rugged has against Crooked. In Rugged's mind, recovering something is better than recovering nothing. Before signing on the dotted line, however, Rugged takes the precaution of looking over the Crooked farm assets more closely. Upon inspection it is revealed that even more equipment is missing and that some of it has actually been stolen by former Crooked farmhands.

Despite all of these problems, Rugged and his wife decide to make the best of a bad situation. They determine that they will invest their own money and apply what they know about farming to fixing, updating, and improving the equipment and outdated techniques. They are hopeful that they will create an awesome new Rugged farm over time and that with new and improved techniques, equipment, and crops, the new farm would be profitable someday.

Rugged's lawyers still do not like this. There is no money in it for them and all too much risk. They reiterate that they want to stay as far away as possible from any share in the Crooked farm assets as they do not want to be remotely involved in any litigation that may arise later. In a move to further disassociate themselves from any potential risks, they send Rugged to other big city lawyers who assist him in structuring a complex asset purchase agreement for being the sole owner of the Crooked assets under the new Rugged farm. By the way, Rugged and his wife pay these new lawyers a rather hefty sum for their services. It takes several weeks for Rugged's new big city lawyers to create this special agreement but at last, the deal is done.

Unbeknownst to Rugged, his contingency fee lawyers should have created what is called a "settlement statement" at this juncture. A settlement statement is a written document clearly stating what the lawyers believe they are owed for their contingency services on the case. This written document must be reviewed, agreed to, and signed by the client to be legally binding. This important step in the lawyer-client relationship is required by The State Professional Rules of Conduct. Furthermore, every lawyer knows about this crucial step as they *swear an oath* to abide by these rules when they earn a license to practice law. These State Professional Rules of Conduct exist to protect clients from predatory lawyers who do not take their sworn oaths to God or country seriously and instead look for ways to take from the very clients they have a sworn duty to protect. ***But Rugged's contingency lawyers do not present any such written statement to Rugged for signing.***

Those familiar with the law might think that Rugged's attorneys were neglecting to furnish the required settlement document for nefarious reasons. Their failure to do so could certainly raise suspicions that they were plotting to see if the risk factors diminished over time or if Rugged managed to raise the value of the farm assets with his hard work. They could then possibly attempt to exact a contingency fee based on a potentially new, higher value of the assets instead of the assets' minimal or possibly even negative value at the time of acquisition. Being able to create confusing and unethical situations like this is exactly why a code of ethics and other rules exist in governing attorney-client relationships. Even though their contract only covered the value of what is collected at the time of their collection, the contingency fee lawyers seemed to secretly be attempting to create a situation tilted in their favor.

Still oblivious to his contingency fee lawyers' potential scheme, Rugged buys some new farmland with a deed in his name and sets up a company to be the Rugged farm entity acquiring the Crooked farm assets. These actions solidify Rugged's role as sole owner of the new farm acquiring the Crooked farm assets, making him the only person responsible should something go wrong. This is just the protection from any future liability associated with the Crooked farm assets the contingency fee lawyers appear to be hoping for. So just before Rugged was to sign the special Crooked farm asset purchase agreement created by the big city farm lawyers, one of Rugged's contingency fee attorneys approaches Rugged and proposes that they own a percentage of the new Rugged farm and become partners with Rugged, providing in-house legal services in exchange for their partnership stake. Rugged is surprised by the suggestion, especially in light of them previously advising Rugged not to have anything to do with the Crooked farm or its assets. Not knowing what to make of the sudden change of heart, Rugged tells the lawyer that he will consider their offer, but he wants to be sure he fully understands it first.

Because the contingency lawyer who spoke to Rugged does not put this new proposal in writing as required by the aforementioned State Professional Rules of Conduct, he seems to continue to hide his ambiguous behavior and efforts to manipulate Rugged. Just as before, the contingency lawyers are obliged to create a written statement reflecting the newly proposed terms. This written statement should give Rugged two options: The first option is for Rugged to pay a dollar amount equal to the contingency percentage of the Crooked farm assets' value at the time that Rugged decides to acquire them from the Crooked farm. The second option is for Rugged to agree, in writing, for the lawyers to become owners of just the contingency fee percentage of those Crooked farm assets that are collected, and *not* the rest of what Rugged is investing to create the new Rugged farm or that new farm itself. Neither option should include the lawyers owning that percent of the newly formed Rugged farm as it was not part of the contingency fee lawyers' collections work. If Rugged selects the second choice, he would be entering into a business relationship with his lawyers. For lawyers to do this, the rules governing such relationships requires them to include a written explanation of the terms and a written warning about how entering such a business relationship with one's attorneys can be very risky because there may be times in such a relationship when the client believes he or she is being objectively represented by their attorney(s), when in reality the lawyers may actually be conflicted representing a business partner. ***Unfortunately, the contingency fee lawyers issue no such written agreement, nor do they even mention the potential conflict of interest.*** Again, this would likely raise the eyebrows of anyone knowledgeable of the law, but Rugged knew little about the law or about the rules that lawyers are sworn to abide by.

Ideally, the contingency fee lawyers should also ask the accounting firm they hired to assess the risks of owning the Crooked farm assets to confirm what the current value of the Crooked farm assets are at this time so that any settlement statement between Rugged and the firm is accurate, but they don't. Given all of their other questionable behavior, it is reasonable to assume that they don't because they know the Crooked farm assets are worthless and they see no reason to pay for an expensive analysis to corroborate what they already know—and because they likely have no intention of creating a written settlement agreement until such time as it is fully to their advantage.

In the event the first year ends quietly without any of the feared risks against the new Rugged farm occurring, those types of risks typically decline. If that were to happen, the contingency fee lawyers would then be in a far better position to try to unethically exact higher fees or an ownership interest even though they had no contractual rights to do so.

In the meantime, the contingency fee lawyers also try to get Rugged to pay them hundreds of dollars an hour to do work that is supposed to be earned as a contingency fee on anything that is collected from suits Rugged levies against some rogue farmhands who he believes stole some of the techniques that are rightfully his as part of the cache of Crooked farm assets. It appears that the greedy contingency fee lawyers want to be paid a handsome hourly sum for this work now and quite possibly be paid again for this work later if something is collected or Rugged agrees to their ownership proposal. Again, these gains would be gotten without assuming any risk or without investing in the new farm's future success, which is not something any farmer or Rugged would knowingly or willingly agree to.

Rugged has no clue how potentially treacherous these lawyers are. Unbeknownst to Rugged, they seem to be lying in wait for the kill as if it is hunting season, and they are poachers on Rugged's land.

After signing the Crooked farm asset purchase agreement, Rugged and his wife get busy fixing the broken farm equipment that the Rugged farm now owns while also working tirelessly to create new farm techniques to make something of the farm itself. Using a variety of old methods, they acquire and new methods they create, they plant, raise, harvest, process, package, advertise, market, and sell the new crops. Rugged learns that the process needs a lot of improvement because the sales do not generate enough profit to pay him. So Rugged and his wife invest in and set up a large test greenhouse where they work extra hours to develop new farm techniques.

While Rugged and his team work diligently building the farm, the contingency fee lawyers work on cases against the rogue farmhands who have allegedly stolen from Rugged. One case looks to be a sure winner as the defendant was prosecuted before for a similar crime against Crooked farmer and the Rugged farm owns a Crooked farm judgment against him. Another case potentially holds the defendants liable to pay Rugged's lawyer's fees should it be proven that they breached their agreement. Because of this fee provision, Rugged's lawyers are willing to accept what is essentially a contingency-based fee payment for this case instead of an hourly fee.

Rugged tries a couple of times to talk to one of the contingency fee lawyers to plan for the future of the farm and its legal expenses as the fee structure is now mixed and at times unclear. He asks the lawyer about the earlier suggestion that the law firm become partners in the farm, providing in-house legal services in exchange for a share in the farm assets. This is an arrangement that appeals to Rugged as the lawyers would be contributing work in the farm the same way that Rugged and his wife are. But the lawyer avoids answering Rugged, saying that he and his partner are at odds about the possibility

Rugged and the contingency fee lawyer continue these conversations periodically without coming to any specific agreement they can put into writing, and the contingency fee lawyers continue working on cases. The one case that looks most winnable starts getting very heated. The big city lawyers claim before the county judge that Rugged's contingency fee lawyers are actually owners in the Rugged farm, and as such shouldn't be allowed to handle defending the Rugged farm as its lawyers. The judge asks Rugged's attorneys if they are, in fact, owners in the Rugged farm in order to clarify the accusations from the other side that they were. This comes as a huge surprise to Rugged as he had no idea that he might have to hire new lawyers if his contingency fee lawyers ever became partners in the farm. Why had the lawyers never mentioned this to him?!

Rugged determines that he must settle this matter immediately. He reaches out to his contingency fee lawyers and asks them once and for all if they are going to become partners or not, and why hadn't they warned him about the risks of the Rugged farm losing them as their legal counsel if they do become partners? The contingency fee lawyers explain to Rugged that such an agreement had to be in writing, and since neither Rugged nor they ever agreed to any details on an ownership proposal, and thus never put one in writing, that no partnership exists between them and they are *not* owners in the Rugged farm. The contingency fee lawyer tells Rugged they will just continue to work on the one rogue farmhand case on a collect attorneys' fees provision basis if they win, and give Rugged a considerable discount on an hourly rate if they lose. They tell Rugged they will send full bills on the Rogue farmhand case now to use in the event they win and direct him to disregard paying them until it the case is over. They continue forward on the other collections case, which is a continuation of the original case under the original contingency arrangement. *This, too, should have been put in writing but the contingency fee lawyers disregard the rule they swore to abide by yet again*. But Rugged, not being a lawyer, didn't know the various rules that his lawyers were supposed to follow.

The contingency fee lawyers tell the county judge under oath that they are not owners in the Rugged farm. They also present a written and sworn statement from Rugged saying that they are *not* and *never have been* owners in the Rugged farm. Rugged believes this ends the conversation about the possibility of having his contingency fee lawyers as partners and he drops the subject completely. The lawyers also drop the issue and continue defending Rugged's farm. After viewing Rugged's and the contingency fee lawyer's sworn statements, the county judge allows the contingency fee attorneys to continue working on the collections case believing their sworn statements that they are not owners.

In the Rogue farmhand case, Rugged's lawyers prove to be no match for the Rogue farmhand's lawyers. After months of bravado, saying that that they should win this case, they are greatly outsmarted and lose miserably. The decision threatens to have a profound impact on other related cases, as the court ruled that that the tools and farming techniques Rogue is using are not the same as the ones Rugged believes they stole from the Crooked farm.

What Rugged finally discovers is that his lawyers have a history of losing more cases than he realized. This particular loss puts Rugged's farm operations in jeopardy and also makes the Rugged farm responsible for having to pay for some or possibly all of the Rogue farmers' lawyers' bills. The Rugged farm is facing ruin. Things are so dire that Rugged's contingency fee lawyers send Rugged to a farm bankruptcy lawyer to prepare for the worst. Staying mentally tough and proactive, Rugged opts to borrow money to cover expenses. Somehow, he, his wife, and their farmhand team are able to pull the farm through it all without filing bankruptcy even though they could have.

In light of their failures and the farm's questionable future, the contingency fee lawyers decide to stop their contingency work entirely, including the work they were doing in the highly winnable case against the former Crooked farmhand who had already been held liable for stealing from the Crooked farm. In attempting to shirk their responsibility, the lawyers finally produce a settlement statement and try to coerce Rugged to sign it and agree to pay them hundreds of thousands of dollars. He objects to the language in it, as it makes him responsible for paying in a way and in an amount that he never agreed to. Much to the lawyers' frustration, Rugged refuses to sign the document. The contingency fee lawyers continue to pressure him and even offer a discount on their fees. When Rugged rejects the statement once more, they threaten to stop work on the most important cases as retaliation. Ultimately, it comes to light that they had not been working on these cases for months already.

Rugged continues to defend the farm by hiring new lawyers. This time he uses the most honest and smart farm lawyers he can find. Rugged and the new attorneys agree that everything must be clearly spelled out in writing before they start working together. A contract is created and signed and work on the major cases continue.

Being honorable, Rugged writes to the contingency fee lawyers and asks them to send a final bill that fairly states what they think is owed to them so he can pay them and completely end their relationship. The contingency attorneys never respond to Rugged nor send him a final bill, so Rugged decides to send them money every month until what he believes is a fair sum for the work completed is paid.

No matter how tough things are now and no matter how tough they were before, Rugged always pays the contingency fee lawyers something even though he pays himself almost nothing. The contingency fee lawyers happily cash all of the checks from the Rugged farm and never send Rugged any final bill or any notice that Rugged owes them more. Over the course of Rugged's relationship with the unethical attorneys, the total payments to them amount to several hundred thousand dollars and Rugged believes he has more than overpaid them. At that point, he stops sending any more checks.

Rugged farm's new honest and smart farm lawyers are very successful. They win cases against some of the farmhands who stole from the Rugged and Crooked farms. Good, ethical lawyers are now protecting the Rugged farm. Years of hard work from everyone on the farm really start to pay off. Due to lots of new seeds and farming techniques developed by the Rugged team, business blossoms. The Rugged farm starts to get incredible recognition. The local paper, as well as state and national farm magazines, call the Rugged farm one of the fastest growing farms in America. Low and behold, once the publicity starts to come out, Rugged's former contingency lawyers show up and demand an ownership piece of the Rugged farm saying it is owed to them because of a previous deal they now claim was made—a deal, by the way that Rugged *never* agreed to, whose terms and risks-warnings do not exist in any document, and *a deal the lawyers actually swore under oath did not exist.*

It is then that Rugged's honest lawyers tell him about the Professional Rules of Conduct all lawyers in the state are required to abide by. Rugged's honest lawyers are embarrassed by their fellow lawyer's behavior and explain to Rugged that these types of lawyers are the primary reason why attorneys are so disliked by the public.

Rugged is dismayed by the contingency fee lawyers' scheme and tells them that they are dishonest, and that they don't keep their word with man or with God. They don't have the integrity to follow the very rules they swore to follow. They didn't create a required written settlement statement. They also neglected to write up an ownership proposal for a portion of the seeds, broken farm equipment, and outdated farming techniques when they were acquired by the Rugged farm. They didn't want to assume the risks of owning any part of the farm during its first year of existence.

Rugged is entitled to react this way. Thank God he is one mentally tough son of a gun. It is almost impossible to fathom that something like this could happen, as Rugged's former contingency fee lawyers are licensed professional advisors whose sworn oaths should have made them trustworthy. Instead, they are willing to do unethical things including lie under oath and bear false witness to try and get *even more money than Rugged had hired them to collect*!

The contingency fee lawyer's nefarious acts and slanderous false claims put Rugged and his wife's life work in jeopardy and threatened the hundreds of Rugged farmhands who built the great Rugged farm. They are bullies who have no scruples. They do not play by the moral rules that govern a fair society, including the rules that govern their own profession, which they swore to comply with. They play by their own corrupt and twisted rules, which seem largely driven by greed.

The lesson of the imaginary Rugged farmer's story is one that looks to educate all farmers that they, too, can be Rugged, and they can learn to stand up and say: **"All of you who look to deceive and bully a Rugged farmer beware, because we are woke to your ways. As Rugged farmers, we know how to separate the wheat from the chaff. And we are willing to wield as sharp a legal scythe in court, separating honorless takers like you from Rugged builders like us."**

I hope that because your eyes are wide open now that you never have an experience like Rugged farmer's. If you become as successful as I wish you to be, then you will certainly face some challenges from people who want what you have without having to work for it. To handle those challenges, you will absolutely have to be mentally tough enough to deal with whatever comes your way. To coach and manage people in ways that inspires, builds confidence, and even strengthens faith, you will have to have a high level of *fortitudo mentis*. The better and bigger the team and business you build, the more mentally tough you will have to be to lead them. Mental toughness should resonate in all aspects of your life and business. It helps you in communications of all types. Start building your mental toughness quotient now and never stop building it. Protect and strengthen yourself by creating your own unique ways to raise your MTQ. Keep raising your MTQ as much and as often as you can because the more success you have, the more mentally tough you will have to be. Mental toughness is a foundational element because building its measure and your measure of success will have a direct and proportional equivalence.

CHAPTER FIVE

FAITH

"Technology is nothing. What's important is that you have faith in people, that they're basically good and smart, and if you give them tools, they'll do wonderful things with them."

—STEVE JOBS

L AST, BUT CERTAINLY NOT LEAST, FAITH IS THE FOURTH ELEMENT required for building a concrete Rugged foundation. It is a centuries-old concept that still puzzles the world because it can be turned on without thinking and just as easily turned off in a flash. Looking at it that way, you could say that everyone has a "faith switch." Most people do not fully know how it is turned on, and no one knows how to absolutely control it. Everyone is able to turn faith on some of the time, but few, if any, can turn faith on all of the time. It is more powerful than any other foundational element a Rugged Entrepreneur can develop when building his or her success. In the same way that you must learn to understand and utilize mental toughness to construct a rock-solid foundation, you have to learn to understand and utilize faith as best as you can. It is a force that everyone experiences and yet it remains difficult to fully comprehend or explain. *How well do you understand your own ability to exercise faith?*

For most individuals, faith is a spiritual concept. Some form of it is found in all religions, but faith is also exercised by people with no religion. For atheists, faith exists as a belief in the absence of any deity or deities. For them there is no God to look to for guidance or to thank. In Islam, faith is known as "Iman," which means to completely submit oneself to God's will. In Hinduism and Buddhism, faith is a concept of knowing one should live in harmony with the world by following the teachings of their religion. In Christianity, faith is an absolute belief in God. The point of all of these different descriptions is to show you how billions of people view the concept differently while also viewing it with great importance in their life. No wonder it is not fully understood by anyone, as man has made it an incredibly confusing subject.

I love to teach entrepreneurs about faith because it can be done in so many different ways, and you would almost always just be scratching the surface of its dynamic impact in the world. When I talk about faith as a foundational element for Rugged Entrepreneurs, I see it as a mental and physical combination—a blending of inner thoughts and outward actions. It can be an incredibly productive tool when building your business. This is *not* a book on my choice of spiritual faith. Any entrepreneur of any religious background can embrace faith the way we look at it here. While I have my own spiritual faith that is deeply important to me, the goal of this chapter is not to address faith as it applies to religion.

I recall the time when I was preparing for a talk before several thousand business owners at a conference in Louisville, Kentucky. The topic was how faith and mental toughness apply to be a successful entrepreneur. I really wanted to help the audience see the vast difference between the concept of belief and the much deeper concept of faith, so I pulled a couple who owned and had built a very successful business together onto the stage. For the sake of this teaching example we will call them John and Linda. I began by asking Linda, "Would you say your husband is a teachable man." She replied, "Oh, most definitely. John has multiple coaches he really listens to about business and life." Knowing both of them were very athletic people, I continued with my questions.

Me
Does your husband like to take on big challenges and learn new things?

Linda
He loves a challenge, especially if it is something new.

Me
Imagine that he comes home one evening very excited and tells you that he has an idea to raise money for a special charity doing something extremely dynamic and dangerous. To pull off this idea he has to learn how to walk a tightrope. By the way, this tightrope will be stretched across two towers that are among the tallest in the United States. Would you think he was just being silly or completely serious?"

Linda
Probably that he was being a dreamer, but also a tad silly.

Me
Okay, what if he then explains that he has always wanted to do this, and that the towers are part of the Time-Warner building in New York City. They are seven hundred and fifty feet high and only about one hundred and sixty feet apart. Would you start to wonder why he knows so many details about the towers and the tightrope walk already?

Linda

I sure would. I would think he was playing some kind of trick or joke on me.

Me

*So right now, you wouldn't believe that he is
going to actually go through with it?"*

Linda

Of course not. He's never walked a tightrope before.

Me

*Okay, let's say that the next day you come home from work and John
is out in the back yard. He's built two small structures about two
feet off the ground and two hundred feet apart. He's also stretched a
tightrope across them. Would you think he was going crazy or that
he was at least serious about learning how to walk a tightrope?*

Linda

*A little bit of both I guess, but I would definitely no longer
think that he was just trying to play a trick on me.*

Me

*All right, let's say he brings you over to look at the structures and he shows
you a book he is reading entitled* Tightrope Walking *for Dummies.
Would you now think he is serious about the whole tightrope thing?*

Linda

A lot more than the day before.

Me

Now, let's say he tells you he has a sponsor who will pay for him to hold the tightrope walking event at the Time-Warner building. Do you start to believe he really is serious?

Linda

Well, he sure seems to be getting more serious each day.

Me

Would you start to worry that he might get hurt or would you just believe that he is going to be a great tightrope walker?

Linda

I wouldn't say I was worried. I would still think it might be some kind of joke.

Me

Let's say a month goes by and he is practicing all day every day and doing exercises to better his balance, all while reading books at night about this skill. Do you believe he can at least learn to walk across the two-hundred-foot-long, two-foot-high tightrope in your back yard?

Linda

Yes, I definitely think he could do that.

Me

*All right, we're making progress. Now, let me ask you again, do you think he could do it or do you **believe** he could do it?*

Linda

I would believe it.

Me

*Do you believe he's ready to head seven hundred and fifty feet up
in the air to tackle walking across the Time-Warner towers?*

Linda

Absolutely not.

Me

*Let's then say you come home the next day and the backyard structures
are now ten feet high. A fall wouldn't kill him, but it could break a bone.
Would you start thinking he is really serious and be a little concerned?*

Linda

Yes, ten feet would concern me a lot.

Me

*Let's say another month passes and he practices walking that tightrope
every day until he can make it across every time without swaying. Would
you say he's successfully learned how to walk the tightrope at that height?*

Linda

Definitely.

Me

*Now, you come home a few days later to find the backyard towers and
tightrope have been raised to thirty feet, which would definitely be high
enough to seriously hurt or kill John if he were to fall. You also notice
another man on the tightrope pushing a wheelbarrow across it while
your husband is watching from below. John calls you over and intro-
duces you to Freddy Nock, the world's record holder for walking a
tightrope 3,000 meters high. He tells you that Freddy is now his coach.
Would you start to realize that your husband is more than serious?*

Linda

Yes, and I would be really worried because he could get seriously injured.

Me

I completely understand. Let's say that he assures you he is going to learn carefully. He tells you he has a burning vision and has to see if he can make it a reality. Do you accept that he's at least going to try to learn how to carry this out successfully at thirty feet?

Linda

Okay.

Me

Another six months pass, and your husband has spent ten hours a day working with Freddy on that thirty-foot-high tightrope. John is walking it like nobody's business, and he can even remain balanced while pushing a wheelbarrow across it. He has also learned to walk it blindfolded. He and Freddy have brought in wind machines to simulate possible weather conditions at the towers' actual height. You ask him, "John, why are you bringing in these wind machines? You're not seriously going to do this at seven hundred and fifty feet high, are you?" And John tells you this is a purpose he is determined to fulfill for the sake of the charity. It is clear from his voice that he has to do it. Do you now start to worry about the seven-hundred-and-fifty-foot-high walk between the Time-Warner towers, or do you just accept it?

Linda

I would now be very worried, and I would be starting to think, "How can I possibly talk him out of this?" I would call his parents and his friends and tell them how worried I am because I don't want to see him dead. I wouldn't want to live without him.

Me

I completely understand, and I would do the same thing if my wife were attempting something that dangerous. But if John were as serious as you've ever seen him be about fulfilling this vision, if he also explained that the reason he and Freddy were practicing pushing a wheelbarrow across the tight rope was because they were planning to add the wheelbarrow to the challenge ... if John also promised you that he was going to focus on working with Freddy for another six months before the event, using a safety cable, and if he further promised that he would let Freddy do the tightrope walk instead of him if Freddy has one iota of doubt about his abilities, would you now believe John was serious about doing it?

Linda

Yes, and I'd still be really worried.

Me

Having seen John learn to walk the tightrope at two feet off the ground and then seeing him master it at thirty feet, do you believe that he can learn to walk it at seven hundred and fifty feet with the help of Freddy and a safety cable?

Linda

Yes.

Me

Okay, do you now **believe** that John will be able to make the walk?

Linda

Yes, I would believe he could.

Me

Perfect, Linda and John, you have both come a long way.

Linda

I said "believe" he could; I didn't say I would want him to.

Me

That's perfectly understandable, but now it's time for the lesson. John comes to you soon after and says, "Linda, I am going to do this with or without your blessing, but I prefer to have that blessing. Do you believe I can do it?"

Linda

*I would tell him yes that I **believe** he could do it.*

Me

John, of course, is excited to have your support and continues working with Freddy on some further height training. It goes so well that Freddy believes John is ready to make the charity walk after just four months of practice. The charity organization sets up the event and television personalities are sent to host the gala. The sidewalks surrounding the Time Warner building are packed with observers who have come to cheer John on. It's a big deal. John is all suited up and ready to make the two-hundred-foot walk across that seven-hundred-and-fifty-foot-high wire. Linda, you are right there on top of the roof with Freddy and the team as they set John up to begin his walk.

IT'S GO TIME.

So now Linda, John looks at you and says, "I am so ready for this. I've done this several thousand times at two feet, thirty feet, and seven hundred and fifty feet. I've also done it millions of times in my mind. Thank you for believing in me." He looks down at the wheelbarrow and adds, "Linda, you have given me that extra belief in myself that I needed to accomplish this. I wasn't being truthful when I said I would do it with or without your blessing. I couldn't have done it without you believing in me. Your belief made me stronger. Now that we are both here, in this moment, at the top of this building, with the crowd *watching, I **know** I can do it and you believe I can too.* **Linda, will you get in the wheelbarrow and ride across the wire while I push?"** **Would you get in the barrel for John to push?**

Linda now understands the difference between *belief* and *faith*. The difference is a big deal and not easy to mentally embrace. Some define belief as "an acceptance or hope in something or someone," whereas faith is more absolute. Faith is the "absence of doubt." In this example, which makes for a great story, Linda can easily believe in John's ability to make the walk, but it would take *faith* for her ride in the wheelbarrow while he pushes it across. I mean, she'd have to have *no doubt*.

It takes a lot of work to accomplish what others think is unimaginable, but faith can propel people to do just that. Do you have the ability to develop the kind of belief that is absent of doubt? The kind of belief that is called faith?

Would it surprise you to know that you already have the ability to turn that faith switch on and off in yourself? Seriously. You'd be amazed by how often you exercise an absence of doubt level of faith in your life on a regular basis. For instance, do you have any doubt that you will continue to breathe once you fall asleep at night? Think about that for a moment. If you had even the slightest concern that you might stop breathing while sleeping, you wouldn't be able to close your eyes!

And how often do you stop to make sure you are still breathing during the day? You don't. You *know* you can breathe. Even though you take thousands of breaths each day, barring a respiratory illness, you never check once to see if you are still doing it.

Need another example? How many muscles and brain activities do you suppose it takes for you to read this book? Your eyeball is a small organ, yet it contains over two million working parts. All of those parts have to function in perfect harmony for you to see as you do. Your eyes are so complicated, here are just a few fun facts that prove their complexity.

- While your fingerprint has about fifty unique characteristics, your eye's retina alone has more than five times that. (Why do you think retinal scanners are used at high-security facilities?)
- Your eye muscles are the fastest muscles in your entire body.
- The cornea, which provides roughly 70 percent of your focus power, is the only tissue in the human body that doesn't contain blood.
- Eyelashes are a bit like sunglasses—they filter the sun's rays. And just like sunglasses you lose them roughly every five months. (The average human sheds approximately one hundred feet of eyelashes over their lifetime!)
- Your eyes have about seven million cones so you can see in color, and about one hundred million cells called "rods," which help you to see better in the dark.
- The only cells that survive from your birth until your death are in your eyes.
- Eye muscles are the only muscles you have that do not need rest to recover and operate at full function. They can be tired, but you won't lose your vision.
- Your eyes play another important role. Some studies suggest that up to 80 percent of your *memories* are developed by the images you see. Studies show that the memory of people who are born blind is different from the memory of people who are born with sight. Those born blind do not have picture dreams when they sleep. People who are born with sight and become blind, can still see in their dreams.

Given the complexity of your eyes and how much they do every second of every day, I would understand it if you stopped many times to check if all two million parts were working right, but you don't. The average person—even those who wear glasses—barely gives it a second thought. We take it on faith that our eyes won't just go on the fritz.

There is a long, seemingly never-ending, list of comparable faith exercises: when you walk around the office, the mall, your neighborhood, or your home, do you ever stop to make sure your heart is still beating? Or do you just trust that it beats without you even being conscious of it? As you go about your day, do you worry that the internal brain function signaling hunger will stop working and that you will starve as a result?

Just as faith (the absence of doubt) enables us to perform miraculous feats, the presence of doubt (fear) can have the complete opposite effect. Those of you with a sports background know exactly what I mean. How often have you heard the following expressions? "If you play not to get hurt, it's more likely that you will." Or, "If you play prevent-defense too soon, the other side is more likely to score." In other words, proceeding with doubt often causes the very thing that you are concerned will happen to happen. The presence of doubt affects *how* and *what* you focus on. It distracts you and ultimately affects your decision-making abilities. It keeps you from maintaining the mindset of abundance and can prompt you to hold on too tightly to whatever you fear losing the most. Focusing on losing something, or on loss itself, trains your mind to see only problems instead of solutions. It diverts your concentration. Under these circumstances, you move slower because your defensive mind is saying, *Look over here. Look over there. Watch out for this. Watch out for that.*

An offensive mind is centered on a more singular action moving forward. Since the focal spectrum is narrower and the effort is concentrated on moving something to the next step, the process from thought to action is more direct, and thus, faster. Think of it this way: when you are being defensive, you have your back turned to what you are protecting, and your mind is thinking only about how the competitor might harm or take away the thing you are protecting. In a business situation, that is like focusing laser-sharp attention on your competition but *not* on your customers. Remember the facts stated earlier about how the parts of your eyes work: 80 percent of your memories (what your mind knows) comes from what you see or have seen. When you are in a *defensive* position (i.e., when you are doubting) your eyes don't see the customer; they see the competition. By contrast, when you are in an *offensive position*, the dynamic is the exact opposite. When you concentrate on what you want to accomplish or gain—such as taking care of or gaining a customer—you can easily see and attend to that customer. Companies that disrupt the marketplace are fast and nimble and generally led by entrepreneurs who focus on the offense, *not* the defense. They are obsessed with customer service and success, *not* with their competitors' actions. ***Are you and your organization "customer obsessed"?***

A Rugged works on understanding and developing faith on four levels: the personal level, the individual or one-on-one level, the group or team level, and the global or organizational level. You have learned that you already possess a personal faith switch. How deeply you develop it and whether it moves from the on or off position are up to you. Looking at some of these different levels more closely may help you grasp the overall concept of faith better.

The personal level is just that—personal. In my private exploration of faith, I have worked on my spiritual side and I have worked on my action-oriented side. On the spiritual side is my faith in God. I love knowing that humans are the one and only entity God made in his image, and also knowing that God has my back. But I have also learned in my life that spiritual principles work whether you embrace religion or not. Spiritual principles such as faith and reciprocity are just like the principles of gravity or relativity. Principles are principles. They are blind to sex, race, religion, or any other label people want to apply to them. Gravity, for instance, works the same for all people, and spiritual principles do as well.

The kind of faith I'm talking about here grows once you learn to embrace it the same way you learn to embrace mental toughness. In many ways, faith and mental toughness overlap. Mental toughness is more about how Ruggeds condition their mind, attitude, work, and communication skills to confront the rigors of day-to-day business. Mental toughness is necessary to make the micro-level strategic moves that allow you to successfully navigate the chessboard of life and business. There are countless calculations involved in supply-chain sourcing, resolving legal entanglements, maneuvering and messaging through market changes, or protecting a company's trade secrets, property, and people, for example. All involve mental toughness. Faith, on the other hand, is the confidence that even with all the unpredictable moves and countermoves that exist in life and business, everything will be all right.

My favorite way to teach personal level faith is through examples of people actually "*taking a leap of faith,*" as the old saying goes. To illustrate how this leap works, let's return for a second to the definition of faith as being the "absence of doubt" and dig a little deeper.

Faith to me is a direct relationship that you have with a force that exists beyond the process of thought. You meet this force when you transcend to the space above or beyond your rational thoughts. There, you are compelled to analyze the likelihood of one outcome or another. The *leap of faith* only occurs when you make the mental jump from a *state of doubting* to *a state of allowing the force to guide you.* To make a leap of faith you are saying to yourself, "I know by not knowing; I choose to believe because I cannot know."

If while walking on a sidewalk from one block to the next you were asked to mentally trace your steps, breaking the distance down into half measurements, you would soon find that the mental calculations are infinite. If the block is one-half mile, then the first half of the walk would have been one-quarter mile. The first half of that first quarter would have been one-eighth of a mile. The first half of that would have been one-sixteenth of a mile. You can keep breaking these distances in half forever, making the task of mapping out all the steps impossible. Faith, in this instance, works in your knowing without a doubt that you can make the walk even if you can't measure all the steps between the start and finishing points. That is what psychologists call the dichotomy paradox. Now, let's look at a real-life business example of this dynamic.

When starting a business or a major project within a business, the job of analyzing every last step one must take to build a comprehensive, foolproof plan is as impossible to calculate as the infinite number of "halved" steps in the sidewalk example would be. People who have not yet become Rugged Entrepreneurs will often drive themselves crazy packing every last detail into their blueprint. Their list grows item by item ad nauseam and ultimately creates a feeling of doubt that the project will ever begin or end. The ongoing list becomes a type of defensive strategy. The person creating it is a lot more focused on preventing or eliminating problems that might arise instead of being focused on creating opportunities and solutions. (We are right back to the concept of being on the offense versus the defense.) It is a trap that dramatically slows one down, and in some cases, even freezes a person in place. The frustration brought on by the growing pile of doubts leaves them unable to move forward. In their mind there will always be more problems to figure out before they can hit the launch button.

A Rugged's personal faith acknowledges that there will always be unforeseen problems while launching a business, and that those problems will come to light and be resolved at some point in the process of making that business a success. Ruggeds have a blueprint before leaping, but it isn't designed to identify every last detail. At some point they trust that they will be able to identify and respond quickly to any unanticipated challenges that come their way. Their faith that the process of engagement will actually reveal the problems that truly need fixing enables them to move the ball forward aggressively and address the issues promptly when they arise. Ruggeds also know that many of the problems imagined in a planner's head are not likely to happen in reality. This is not to say that Ruggeds move forward with reckless abandon. The planner without faith is focused only on worst-case scenarios and all the details to avoid them, while Ruggeds with faith trust that their analytical skills and instincts will keep the customers' needs top of mind and will also help them successfully find ways to meet those needs. That faith is linked to the Rugged Intellect we discussed earlier.

Rugged Entrepreneurs are great at building disruptive and fast businesses because they learn to act on their Rugged Intellect with *faith*. Faith, and the actions stemming from it, enable Ruggeds and their companies to move much faster than other leaders in corporate and professional environments where long experimental trials and hierarchy exist. Waiting for answers from higher ups, being constricted by complex corporate reporting structures, and overanalyzing probabilities to reach consensus slow things down.

Steve Jobs sums up the power of the "leap of faith" approach in two great quotes: *"The doers are the major thinkers. The people that really create the things that change this industry are both the thinker and doer in one person."* And, *"You can't connect the dots looking forward; you can only connect them looking backwards. So, you have to trust that the dots will somehow connect in your future. You have to trust in something: your gut, destiny, life, karma, whatever. This approach has never let me down, and it has made all the difference in my life."*

This same type of personal faith is also necessary to be a strong team builder. As I was becoming a Rugged Entrepreneur, I had to learn to trust my ability to quickly assess and judge people while interacting with them. That entailed studying their past work results along with what I could read as their current skills and weaknesses when they worked on their own and in teams. In society the word "judge" is somewhat frowned upon. This is especially so in the "churchy" world where religious group-think dictates that you "judge not lest you be judged." But a Rugged's judgment comes from objective study and hard work such as reading books, listening to successful people, working on and solving problems as a team member, and imparting all of the necessary skills as a team leader. With time and practice, personal faith enhances a Rugged's ability to see how people will bond and work together, even though logic suggests that it's impossible to know all of their traits and how a group of very dissimilar individuals will collaborate effectively as a unit.

Rugged Entrepreneurs learn to faithfully build teams that collaborate, solve problems on the move, and anticipate what customers will want or need often before the customers know. They learn to build teams that communicate at high and constructive enough levels to accept personal responsibility faster, to act faster, to engage faster, and as such, to grow faster.

Entrepreneurs who cannot develop and exercise this type of personal faith (i.e., some corporate or professional entrepreneurs) are better suited for more specific entrepreneurial jobs within an organization where the word team is just a way to name a group that works in the same place.

As you have already gathered, I believe Steve Jobs was one of the greatest Ruggeds of all time. I feel compelled to repeat one of my favorite business quotes from him as it applies here as well. *"Great things in business are never done by one person. They're done by a team of people."* Is it any wonder that this man knew how to build products people wanted before they even knew they wanted them? Steve Jobs had great faith in his team-building skills. He had great faith that the dots would ultimately connect and that not every one of them had to do so at the planning stages. He knew how to be a thinker and a doer all in one. He had faith that his teams would work incredibly well together to innovate and launch all of the amazing goods and services they did, and that they would improve these goods and services with every new iteration!

Of course, we have just scratched the surface in this lesson on faith development, so please do not beat yourself up if it takes time to figure out how to keep the faith switch on as much as you possibly can. In the crazy intricate world of being a Rugged Entrepreneur engaged in a challenging game of business chess on a daily basis, there will always be doubts. The key is knowing how powerful faith can be and continuing to work on fostering it within yourself and your organization. Start by working with this dynamic personally and then extend what you've learned about your own faith to other levels of your operation. This is often the most powerful element in any Rugged's foundation.

After understanding some of the dynamics of personal faith and the importance of building it, Ruggeds can intentionally begin instilling faith into the individuals they work with, their teams, and ultimately, in their organization as a whole. I will admit that it is not as easy to help adults grow and tap into their faith as it is to teach young children. I will never forget taking our son and daughter to Universal Studios in Orlando, Florida, for the first time. Aaron was ten years old and Hayley was seven. One of the attractions was based on the 1996 Steven Spielberg movie *Twister*. When we finally made it to the front of the line, we were positioned on a platform overlooking a set that was an exact replica of the movie set. Filmed images of a tornado were projected on a background screen as gusts of wind created by the special effects team swirled all around us.

When the fans creating these gusts of wind were turned nearly all the way up, I looked at Aaron and Hayley and told them that this was the most realistic amusement park experience ever built. I grabbed hold of the railing in front of us, which was designed to keep riders from moving too far forward into the gale force, and explained to the kids that the rail was there as a safety precaution so they wouldn't be swept up by the tornado. Daphene caught on instantly. She knew that I was using humor to raise the level of excitement for the kids. She grabbed the rails, too, and said something like, "That wind is really picking up!" A slight look of terror crossed Hayley's face before she grabbed the rail as well. Her grip was so tight you could see her knuckles turn white. Aaron reached out and grabbed the rail right after her. As the wind sounds grew louder, an image of a cow flew by on the background screen. Heightening the energy, I yelled, "Hang on, here it comes!" Hayley immediately cried, "Hold on to me, Daddy!" so I wrapped an arm around her and held the rail with my other hand while Daff did the same with Aaron. With their eyes clenched shut and their mouths still wide open from screaming, the tornado passed and the gusts from the fans gradually died down. When the experience came to an end and the lights were raised again, the kids realized it was just another special effects attraction and nobody was in any real danger of getting blown away.

For a brief moment, though, they had absolute faith that we could all be carried up into the air by those winds just like the flying cow was. The faith of a child is a powerful thing to behold. If only it were as easy to stir in us as adults.

So many entrepreneurs don't understand what is involved in helping individuals tap into and exercise faith. Some are micromanaging, detail-obsessed perfectionists who check everything to make certain it is right according to their own preferences. Some are egocentric control freaks who derive power by exerting their authority over other people. Others are happy- go-lucky, backslapping cheerleaders who overpraise the people they are training or leading, which only gives those trainees or followers a false sense of confidence, not a sense of faith at all. All of these personality types attempt to control others in their own way and sometimes for their own purposes.

To help develop an individual's faith in themselves so they can be the high-level performer they are meant to be, Ruggeds learn to let go of that control. The best of them use what is referred to as *expectant* mental toughness. In fact, every great coach that I have ever studied understands the concept of expectancy and what it does to actually raise an individual athlete's faith and performance level. They are clear about what they hope to see from their athletes and clear that, although the bar they set is high, their expectations are still very achievable. They also give feedback that is honest. Of course, "expectant coaching" is a lot more difficult than just saying the right words. It involves guidance up to the point where you can truly let go and trust that great things will follow in great ways. Expectant coaching has its own language and you need to be a serious student of psychology to understand that language well.

The coach I've enjoyed studying the most is Coach K (Mike Krzyzewski) of Duke basketball lore. He has mastered more than winning games as a player and coach; he has mastered the art of effective "program building." This is a way of coaching that extends to everyone and every aspect of an organization. It produces championship players, championship teams, championship coaches, and champion-caliber *people*. And by the way, it builds rabid fans too. Coach K is so legendary for this ability that the Olympic committee turned to him after the U.S. basketball team suffered its worst performance in its history at the 2004 games. After dominating the sport in every Olympic competition since 1992, the 2004 U.S. team—which had pros playing, not just amateurs—barely managed to take home a bronze medal. They clearly needed an overhaul from someone such as Coach K. He was asked to restore Team U.S.A. to its former Gold status and build a program that would keep it there. Every Rugged should read Coach K's book *The Gold Standard* because the lessons he teaches about program building will prove vitally important in your organizational faith-building efforts too. One point I will mention here is that he always singled out players at each practice for personal interaction, communication-building exercises, and edification. In another of Coach K's books, *Leading from the Heart*, he addresses this same skill. He writes that he intentionally studies and gets to know the personalities of every player he works with. Being a good expectant coach, whether to an athlete or a business team member, requires this high level of detail and attention to psychology. Expressing personal interest in your people triggers and builds their faith in themselves. This is not something that someone who is lazy can pull off. You cannot compliment an athlete or a team member idly. That leads to overpraising and sets low and misdirected expectations. It requires a serious time investment to do this well. Coaching faith into someone requires learning how each player is wired and figuring out how to push buttons in a way that best suits that player. The right buttons for that individual's personality will bring out the best responses from them. The more successful the responses are, the greater the player's faith in him- or herself becomes.

So how well do you know your key people? And how much time have you spent learning about the psychology of different personalities?

In addition to Coach K's books, I recommend that you read two really good psychology books that can help you develop the skills to analyze yourself and your key people. Having these skills can be a game changer as you proceed to foster faith in your people. The author of both books is Florence Littauer. The first, which is titled *Personality Plus*, provides an in-depth study of the different personalities types that exist and includes a test to determine yours. The second, which is titled *How to Get Along with Difficult People*, might be better called *You Are Difficult, But This Is How to Get Along with Others Anyway*. You should read *Personality Plus* first so you can learn about your own dominant and sub-personalities, and the same for other individuals you are coaching. The second book imparts professional analytical skills that I believe can enhance communication and enable you to work with others on a very high level. These books will *not* teach you how to be an expectant faith-building coach, but they will provide you with the personality analysis skills necessary to become one.

In addition to encouraging leaders to know the personalities of the individuals with whom they are working, Coach K emphasizes that there is no such thing as treating everyone the same out of some sense of fairness. He expects his players to make good choices on and off the court. He also expects them to earn respect, and he readily admits that those players who have earned greater levels of respect are treated differently than those who have not. For example, he makes a comparison between All American Grant Hill and many of the new freshman players. He says that if the team is leaving for a game and a freshman player is five minutes late, the bus will be gone by the time that player arrives. On the other hand, if senior All American Grant Hill is five minutes late, Hill will get a phone call from one of the assistant coaches while two others set out to try to find him. It's clear to me that in this example Coach K is illustrating how building an atmosphere of expectancy works. People are *not* treated equally, and everyone understands and knows it. In Coach K's championship environment, there is earned credibility and respect and there is the lack of it.

You have to be mentally tough to be an expectant coach. After taking the test in Littauer's book, the results indicated that I have equal parts of two personality types. Fifty percent of me is "sanguine" and 50 percent of me is "choleric." If you want to know what that means, you will have to read *Personality Plus*. But I will say this: the sanguine side of me wants people to be happy and to like me. This was something I had to work on in order to instill faith in my people and to get them to stretch to their highest capabilities. We don't always like people when they are pushing us hard to be our best. We may grow to appreciate them later, but when we're in the thick of being challenged, liking the person driving us is probably not the first emotional response we'll have. In today's politically correct world, with fairness doctrines of every kind running rampant, it is more difficult than ever to be an expectant coach. If you do not develop the psychoanalytical wisdom offered in the aforementioned books, and you do not develop the mental toughness required to be an expectant coach, it will severely lessen your ability to develop faith in the individuals on your teams.

Great teams are made up of good to great talents coming together in unison for a singular purpose. You have to expect good to great talent to do good to great work. You can overlook or turn mistakes into positives as appropriate. In fact, you should even expect mistakes, as it means that people are taking enough aggressive action to push growth forward. But ultimately, you have to expect the final work to be something great. Edify and encourage people when they do something really well, but never praise them simply for praise's sake. Do not give performance bonuses or raises unless the person or team performs the way that they are expected to perform and the way they agreed to perform. Not having good to great expectations is like saying you don't have strong faith in their abilities. Your capacity to instill faith in an individual has a direct correlation to how real your praise is. If you praise people for par or subpar work results, then your praise—be it in the form of a verbal compliment, a reward, or both—will not be taken as seriously as it should. That diminishes your ability to instill and build faith in others.

Have you ever watched a football team run out the clock? When there is less than a minute before halftime and a coach tells the offense to do that instead of forcefully getting within scoring range, they are sadly "playing not to lose"—and worse, they are doing the very opposite of instilling faith in their team. Being a North Carolina State graduate, I have seen two football coaches make calls to run out the clock on a regular basis. One of those, Tom O'Brian, lost a tied game on a last-second punt return in 2012. A soon-to-be NFL quarterback, Mike Glennon, was NC State's leader and he had put up an amazing game. Glennon was 29 for 62 with 467 yards and had been consistently tearing the UNC Tarheels up. He had led the Wolf Pack team from a twenty-one-point deficit to a lead. UNC tied the game on a field goal with about three minutes left to play. Instead of voting with confidence in his future NFL QB with a hot hand and aggressively attempting to score with a two-minute throwing drill, O'Brian decided to play safe and run the ball. He called three running plays, which were all stuffed, then punted with about a minute left. On the punt, UNC scored a touchdown to seal the game. Playing not to lose when you have great talent is not the way a Rugged operates. It is certainly *not* a vote of confidence, and it is *not* an example of expectant coaching.

O'Brian was fired after that season. It's very telling that NC State lost over 1,000 season ticket holders and almost a million and a half dollars in revenue during his tenure. Play calling that does not reflect aggressive faith in your players is a confidence killer. It affects the individual, the team, and the outcome of any goal they undertake together. John Wooden certainly had a different strategy. He, and all other great coaches, almost always played to win. A conservative approach such as the one O'Brien took clearly spreads to the fans, too, as North Carolina

State University's athletic director discovered when she looked at attendance and season ticket holder declines over the six years NC State had a conservative coach.

A great definition of faith can be found in that oldest of books I refer to as *Basic Instructions Before Leaving Earth*. In it, faith is defined in a unique way: ***"Now Faith is the substance of things hoped for, the evidence of things not seen."*** Much like a mathematical equation, you can only arrive at the sum of faith when both parts of this definition are present. Many scholars say that there are two types of faith—the first is *growing faith* and the other is *absolute faith*. We talked about this before in the example of our tightrope walker, but we did so in slightly different terms. There we explored the difference between *belief* and *faith*. What the preceding definition confirms is that faith is neither one thing nor the other; it is both. It is my sense that belief becomes faith; growing faith becomes absolute faith; and as this quote suggests, things unseen become things of substance. Let's look, for a moment, at the second half of this wonderful definition: "the evidence of things not seen." In the context of my writing this book, my faith began with a simple idea. The idea, of course, was *unseen* as it incubated in my brain. After I verbalized the idea to others, it was heard, but it was still not visible. It was in the process of becoming. Now let's look at the first part of the definition: "the substance of things hoped for." Again, in the context of this book, it could be said that the "substance" was the physical and mental work I did as I committed my thoughts to paper. And the thing "hoped for" was the very book you now hold in your hands.

When you understand faith in this way—as an active, transformative process that begins with an idea that is vocalized, then given substance, and finally manifested into reality—you begin to see how faith can potentially bring forth productivity and success in your organization. Thoughts and spoken words by themselves have no substance, but they are the starting line to exercising faith.

I will admit that I talked about writing this book for more than five years. The longer I talked about it but did nothing to get the ball rolling, the less people believed I would ever do it. We have all heard the expression "all talk and no action." That was me at the time. But once I told people that I had started writing this book and had a certain number of pages completed, they began to believe me again. This is very important to note: you cannot be afraid to verbalize your vision to others, but you must be willing to do the work that gives your idea substance. You must put in the time and energy that enables your idea to materialize and that finally evidences what you had hoped for from the very beginning. Teaching this definition to people really helps them build faith, provides a blueprint for exercising it, and enables them to accomplish great things too.

An organizational community with the combination of a fervent work ethic, a humble and healthy pride, mental toughness, and the high faith quotient we are talking about is unbeatable.

The New England Patriots have long been an organization that reflects this kind of culture. If players don't rise up and to do their job by possessing all of the preceding qualities, they quickly move out. It is a huge factor in the team being a football dynasty for so long.

People support organizations like this because they have faith in them, and they are rarely disappointed. Customer satisfaction in a business can generate the same kind of faith and devotion among your clients as winning teams generate amongst their fans. *Wouldn't you love to have the kind of loyalty Pats fans have for their team?*

Coach K sees the same dynamic with Duke's fans who are affectionately called "Cameron Crazies." He has said that they are like "the team's sixth player on the court." The school and its fans in the Raleigh-Durham area could easily fill a sixteen- to twenty-thousand-seat arena, and Duke could afford the cost to build such a large place. But Coach K is adamant about the team staying in that relatively small arena so that the presence of their diehard fans will always be heard and felt. He knows building a bigger, more modern stadium would make the school millions of dollars more in revenue, but he also knows the value of the fans' enthusiasm for his team. Your customers, just like sports fans, can serve as your home field advantage too. If Ruggeds build a business with as solid a foundation, using the four elements we have just discussed in great detail, they will also have a winning organization with customers who are proud to do business with them and who will cheer through all stages of your organization's growth and success.

But as every Rugged knows, such a culture does not come to fruition quickly. It is built over time. All four of the elements must be well cultivated. Once the foundation is built right, it can be consistently maintained and even expanded upon. I must say that faith is the most difficult foundational element to perfect, but it is also the most powerful. Companies with organizational faith compete more confidently in the marketplace. They have less turnover, create more opportunity, develop employees who work with an ownership mentality, make breakthroughs that keep them evolving ahead of the competition, survive and even grow through economic downturns, and are often discussed in a fabled way by industry insiders. Because their excellent reputation precedes them, they always have an easy time on-boarding talent and cultivating it from within. That benefit alone gives them a tremendous advantage against other organizations. Start building your organizational faith now.

PART II

RUGGEDIZING
FOR MARKET
DISRUPTION

CHAPTER SIX

RUGGED SIGHT

"The only thing worse than being blind is having sight but no vision."
—HELEN KELLER

WHILE DEVELOPING THE FOUR ELEMENTS OF A RUGGED FOUNDA-tion should be your highest priority so that your "skyscraper" can always weather the storms of business and stand tall in the field of competitors, there are some additional qualities that set Ruggeds apart from others and ideally equip them for becoming the market disruptors they hope to be. In learning to build teams and move a company fast, the first of these qualities is Rugged Sight, and pardon the pun, it is something I wouldn't want you to overlook. This quality is vital as you venture to build each new story atop of the amazing foundation you are already in the process of creating. I mention it now because it is never too early in your Rugged process to begin developing it.

Before I define Rugged Sight for you, I invite you to contemplate the following statements, as unrelated as they may seem at first glance.

- Humans have more than five senses.
- You do not lose more heat from your head than you do from any other part of the body.
- Gum does not stay in your digestive system for longer periods of time than other food.
- Your hair and nails do not continue to grow when you die.
- Mt. Everest is not the tallest mountain; Mauna Kea is taller from base to tip.
- The Great Wall of China is not visible from outer space.
- Bats are not blind.
- Ostriches do not stick their head in the sand.
- Dogs are not color-blind.
- Lemmings do not make suicide pacts and kill themselves by jumping off cliffs *en masse*.

Are you surprised by any of these statements? Each of them is true, although people frequently think the opposite. This list illustrates just how easy it is to have previously heard or read something and believe it to be factual even when it is not.

Rugged Sight enables you to have a highly accurate view of the world. Many times, it even allows you to see what the world could potentially be. That is what market disruptors do best. When Rugged Sight is especially well developed, it combines critical thinking with the ability to explain complex thoughts in a very simple way that makes perfect sense to those who need to hear it. From the mouths of Ruggeds, these complex thoughts seem like common sense.

Having Rugged Sight provides an incredible advantage in a world of constant decision-making. All business owners make decisions, but Ruggeds tend to have to make a lot of them and with a greater degree of consideration. Having Rugged Sight gives Rugged Entrepreneurs a competitive edge. It enables them to make advancements and improvements, to effect immediate and considerable change in the marketplace and to work better with others.

Critical thinking is said to be a concept that is at least several thousand years old, dating back to Socrates. But I imagine that earlier cultures, including the ancient Chinese culture, had plenty of leaders who were adept at critical thinking. Socrates often gets the credit because of his process of training students in debate. This process, known widely today as the Socratic method, engages individuals in a form of collaborative argument. Socrates basically taught his students by having them question current beliefs and ideologies to help differentiate what they *thought* from what they *knew* as truth. By encouraging them to rely on facts, he helped them to be more informed.

No matter who gets the credit, critical thinking is a skill that can be strengthened if an individual chooses. A person using it learns to think in a more organized and rational way. This results in making more logical connections. The last time most people intentionally sharpened their critical thinking skills was when they were in high school or college. For Ruggeds, however, critical thinking is involved in almost all of their daily decisions, from the smallest and simplest to the most complex ones. A Rugged knows his or her choices affect people. A Rugged sees in advance how their actions impact what is accomplished when team members work collaboratively with one another and when they are at odds with one another too.

Having Rugged Sight empowers an entrepreneur to do two things very well. One is what I call "playing business chess" and the other is what I call "organizing chaos." Playing business chess involves short- and long-term strategic thinking, while organizing chaos is a Rugged's ability to organize beneficial outcomes from chaos that happens naturally or chaos created intentionally to stir things up so people respond differently to their situation. It works to advance people, teams, processes, ideas, projects, and organizations.

Playing Business Chess

There are all manner of ways to enhance your Rugged Sight and to train your eye to see the whole business chessboard and beyond. I take this subject so seriously that I put objects in my surroundings (as discussed in chapter four on mental toughness), to continuously remind me to think critically. In that chapter I pointed out two artworks that hang in my office: *The Son of Man* and *Two Indian Horses*. *The Son of Man* is a 1964 painting by the Belgium artist René Magritte that I first saw and became curious about after watching the 1999 movie *The Thomas Crown Affair*. *Two Indian Horses* is a painting by Bev Doolittle, who is an American artist specializing in camouflage technique (the painting style in which certain elements can be viewed more than one way). Both pieces spur and condition me to critically assess and view the things in front of me *and* the things that are hidden.

The Son of Man depicts a gentleman in a bowler hat standing before a sea wall on a partly cloudy day. A big green apple floats directly in front of his face. In the movie *The Thomas Crown Affair*, the main character hires actors who are all dressed as the character in this painting, except that each actor also carries a briefcase. He directs these actors to wander in and out of the halls of the museum; they are intended to cause a distraction. They roam around in plain sight of the visitors and the guards, while the main character returns a piece of stolen art and pilfers a new piece in its place. He does this knowing that the police and the woman he loves are both watching on security cameras. In the end, the police come out of hiding and round up all of the characters. As the officers make the actors open their briefcases, hundreds of printed copies of *The Son of Man* painting spill out from inside. The painting itself is often described as generating a conflict in thought, focusing on what is seen verses what is not seen. In the movie, this is the exact point the art thief wishes to make to his adversaries and the woman he loves. His actions beg the questions:

- Do you focus on what is right in front of you?
- Or do you focus on what is beyond that which is right in front of you?
- What are you missing when you focus on one versus the other?

In business, there is always a list of priorities. It is natural to want to attend to the ones right in front of you. It must be noted, however, that when an entrepreneur hyper-focuses on those priorities, he or she could be missing things that are *not* right in front of them—things that may be or could potentially become equally or more important than the ones right in front of them at any given moment.

The painting *The Son of Man* makes me intentionally think about the things in front of me while simultaneously asking myself critical questions about them and what I might be missing when I focus so intently on them. These questions include:

- What are the unintended or unforeseen consequences—good or bad—that could come from the things I might be missing if the thing I am working on in the forefront goes off course?
- Who or what would benefit or be hurt?
- How could what I am focusing on be done better?
- What could go wrong because I failed to see something that might happen in the future or something that is happening in the present but is hidden from my immediate view?

The painting is a constant reminder that I do not see everything about what is right in front of me, nor do I see all of the things that my focus keeps from my immediate sight. This critical analysis provokes me. It helps me clearly see and play out all—or at least, many—of the steps I need to take regarding whatever we are working on at the time.

A great individual or group exercise you can use to explore this further involves writing or projecting a list of problems on a whiteboard or screen in the front of the room. From where people are sitting, have them hold a hand up in front of their face with their fingers spread so there are gaps that they can see through. They should have a direct view of the list in the front of the room. Tell them to focus on the list without moving their hand and see if they can read it. (They should be able to.) Then tell them to close their eyes for a few seconds and when they open them, this time they should focus on their fingers directly in front of their face. What you and they will discover is that when you focus on the fingers right in front of you, you can no longer see the list of problems clearly enough to read it. This exercise illustrates how we often see only what we focus on. Even though both things are right in front of us, one is more focal than the other. You can only see the one your eyes are trained on; you cannot see both at the same time.

Although it could be, this is not just an exercise to say that if you focus on your problems, all you will see are those problems and not the solutions right in front of your face (i.e., your own hands). I believe in staying positive and optimistic, but I also agree with forcing yourself to think critically and see any challenges that might come up in the course of moving a person, project, team, or organization forward. This kind of critical thinking helps you analyze the worst-case scenarios and decide if and how you would deal or possibly recover from them should they arise. As a project advances forward in time and production, the possible outcomes are always changing and in need of reanalyzing. When the worst-case scenarios you can think of are manageable, you can make decisions and cope using workarounds that still help you to move forward. We have all heard the saying "shoot for the stars and if you reach the moon, you will have accomplished more than most."

The Bev Doolittle painting *Two Indian Horses* depicts a U.S. Cavalry soldier guarding a string of horses in a snow-covered forest. The scene is predominately painted in whites and shades of brown. The Cavalry soldier stands out, distracting the viewer's eyes. When people come into my office and look at the picture hanging on the wall, I will sometimes ask them, "Why do you think the painting is named *Two Indian Horses*? More often than not, they will peer at it for a while and ask me if it is about the horses having been trained by or taken away from Indians. But a closer look actually reveals two crouching, camouflaged Indians taking the two horses on the far left away. They are difficult to spot but once you see them, you automatically understand the painting's name.

This picture hangs diagonally to my *The Son of Man* picture. While *The Son of Man* print is there as a reminder to generally think about all of the things in the forefront and background of my business life, *Two Indian Horses* is a more specific reminder that there are always things lurking in the world that could cause one loss. The sooner you discover them, the better off you will be.

Over a lifetime of experience in the business world, I have witnessed and experienced so much loss that could have been foreseen and averted with stronger and faster critical thinking. Failing to call out the actions of would-be thieves, be it employees or so-called advisors in various service industries who exaggerate their billable hours or intentionally create confusion because they can get away with it, is a mistake that can cost a Rugged dearly. In my business lifetime, I have spent a small fortune in money and time working with bad actors who took advantage of me or the situation I was in longer than I should have allowed. The sooner you can identify those who would wrongfully take from you and make appropriate changes, the better off you will be.

The practice of lying and stealing on a regular basis is not a practice exclusive to the particular breed of unethical attorneys or service providers I've encountered. Swindlers also come in the form of employees, customers, and outsiders. Laziness, lying, and thievery are the three things I abhor the most. Those who steal are the laziest beings of all. A boxed fruitcake from a famous fruitcake company sits on my desk. I keep it there because of a story I heard about that famous company. They were almost forced to close their business because their controller embezzled millions of dollars from them. I call the one on my desk "the million-dollar fruitcake," and it's there to remind me of the cost a business can incur when you don't pay enough attention to the details or think analytically. That fruitcake and the painting *Two Indian Horses* are warnings that not seeing things in advance can cost me, and those depending on me, dearly. There are always pitfalls and people ready to cause a problem or take something you or your team worked hard to build. It's up to you to be vigilant and develop Rugged Sight so they do not succeed.

Of course, just by being Rugged, you understand that you cannot think of or foresee every possible set of problems and work them out beforehand. You can, however, condition your critical thinking skills to perform at a level where you see more of the possible problems quicker than those who barely even look for them at all. Those with lesser critical thinking skills often take a leap of faith only to fail miserably because they had not trained their Rugged Sight. As we discussed earlier, a leap of faith is often necessary, but not without the kind of proper preparation that, let's say, our tightrope-walking friend from an earlier chapter undertook.

Critical thinking is a form of preparation for just about everything. It works like a computer program to which you can always tweak and add speed and efficiency. The more you exercise and work on your critical analysis skills, the faster you can process complex ideas, actions, personalities, possibilities, the competition, others' perceptions, how their words align with their actions, how inspired or frustrated those around you are, how your decisions and the decisions of others flow together ... the list goes on and on. You must intentionally work on your critical thinking skills to string all the data and experiences together quickly enough to make good decisions. Our organizations are known for their speed because we develop leaders that have great critical thinking skills and we empower them to make capable decisions.

Critical thinking is so important that it should be developed into a habitual skill you continuously improve upon. By habitual, I mean that it becomes something that is always operating in the background of your mind. I start almost every day giving thanks for what I get to do and for the skills I've developed to do it. I then follow that time reading and meditating to improve my critical thinking and to make sure that the switch in my mind to fire it up is turned on and operating at full capacity. As that skill became more and more of a habit for me, I noticed that it empowered me to get better results faster. It enabled me to work with more projects and more people at the same time without being over-whelmed. Habitual skills work like the Windows operating system. You can have multiple skills on and running simultaneously while you go about getting things done. And you can access these skills interchange-ably without distraction or taking time out.

Critical thinking is so important to building a business that it prob-ably shouldn't be called "critical thought." The negative connotation of the word "critical" is that it is "disapproving" or "judgmental." Of course, in our context it means "evaluative" or "analytical" thinking. To be clear, though, I look at it as "complete thinking."

In my mind, this term best describes the intentional thought processes we are talking about. Complete thinking is a method of powering through until much of the important mental analysis is done swiftly and as many of the possible variables you can think of have been explored. This process reviews a project in advance to see whether it will produce results as good or as bad as expected, worse than expected, or better than expected.

Looking at the skill this way, you can see how it plays an important role in playing business chess. Critical or complete thinkers are far better equipped for success in business. All Rugged Entrepreneurs know they must develop this skill one way or another.

A big part of acquiring it comes from the pain of failure. The other part comes from studying and digesting wisdom in all of its facets. To repeat something we have already discussed because it is worth a reminder in this context: studies about millionaires and billionaires almost always reveal that they have voracious reading habits. Studies also reveal that they are students of people, business, strategy, thought, and the process of how things work and affect the industries they operate in. To play business chess well, a Rugged must develop their Rugged Sight so they can make the kinds of short- and long- term strategic moves that lead to success. A business, and the atmosphere it operates in, is constantly changing, so there are always strategic moves to be considered and made. One of the reasons I am a serial Rugged Entrepreneur is the challenge and thrill that playing business chess always presents.

Organized Chaos

Now, please, do not think for a moment that an oxymoron or the analogy to a chess game means that this is not serious business. Entrepreneurs accept the responsibility of actions that can potentially impact a great number of people, whether they are employees, customers, vendors, or anyone else touched by their organization in some way. One who does not take that responsibility seriously will likely be out of business rather quickly. Building businesses also comes with the opportunity to create incredible opportunities for people, especially when a Rugged Entrepreneur becomes skilled at leaning into or creating chaos and then organizing its powerfully disruptive nature.

I love being a Rugged Entrepreneur as it is more challenging and rewarding than anything else I could have chosen. I have known so many people who've had great careers but after twenty to thirty years, have become stagnant or disconcerted. Their top priority is what is often called "walking the green line"—a reference to an advertising campaign done by Fidelity Investments. This expression basically means they are waiting for their investment strategies to pay off so they can retire.

I, fortunately, have never felt this way. In fact, most of my business interests today center around helping people become Rugged Entrepreneurs because it brings a similar challenge and thrill to both parties—myself and them. While I have seen this thrill take hold of people hundreds of times, in the last few years I have particularly enjoyed watching it in one of my best friends. His decision to stop walking the green line and leave the corporate world not only changed his life, it changed the lives of his two sons and his wife in a fantastic way.

Jim Wilson was one of several athletic and smart sixth-grade friends I made when we started playing golf together at the Asheville Municipal Golf course one summer many years ago. There were several other young golfers whose parents learned that they could drop their children off at the course all day for about five dollars. We would get a Coke and a hotdog for lunch and play as much as we'd like. After thirty-six holes we would either have putting contests for dimes or go peruse the creeks and woods around the course to find lost golf balls and sell them back to the course manager for about twenty cents each. Our parents would pick us up at around six o'clock on their way home from work. There were no cellphones and no worries in those days. Our folks just trusted that we were okay out in the world on our own. In high school Jim played baseball and basketball and was also one of the top-ranked students in our class. As I mentioned, he went to the University of Tennessee next. There, he got an electrical engineering degree.

Jim then went to work for Raytheon after graduating college. He married his wife, Leigh Ann, who also went to high school with us and attended the University of Tennessee a year after Jim started there. While working for Raytheon, Jim got his MBA at East Tennessee State University and he and Leigh Ann began their family of two sons, Tyler and Kyle. Shortly after earning his MBA, Jim went to work for Eastman Chemical (formerly Eastman Kodak) where he had an illustrious twenty-seven-year career advancing through the company in roles ranging from construction to sales and ultimately to sourcing. He reached one of the highest positions in the multibillion-dollar organization as its Director of Global Procurement. All went well there for Jim, though he later admitted that his final years at the company were no longer challenging for him. By the end, his job ceased being the source of passion it once was. At some point, he started calculating the exact number of days before he believed he would be able to exit. He played golf regularly at the local country club, and he and Leigh Ann greatly enjoyed watching their sons grow up as they counted down the days to being able to walk away from the corporate confines.

Jim and I worked together when we were in high school, and I ate dinner at his house almost as much as I did at my own. His mom was one of the best cooks in the world, and she loved Jim wholeheartedly. Although we went to different colleges, we stayed in touch and I always told Jim that he would be the CEO at Eastman one day. That is how much I believed in his potential. As my experiences in Rugged Entrepreneurialism started to result in a high level of success, I was able to help coach other entrepreneurs. At the time that Jim was fantasizing about retirement, one of my favorite pupils, Brandon Kinder, decided to go Rugged and start a business while simultaneously working as a pharmaceutical rep earning a six-figure income. Brandon called me from time to time for business coaching. I always thought that his ideas, along with his *rare-air* work ethic and coachability, made him someone who'd be great to build a large company with one day. As it happened, Brandon and I discussed the prospect of scaling his business as a franchise, which is exactly what one of the companies I founded is designed to do. Brandon's company was chemical in nature and centered around today's cutting-edge microbial disinfecting services. Before acquiring Brandon's company to position it for scaling, my Rugged Sight served its purpose. I began thinking about all the ways taking Brandon's business to the next level could work. Jim Wilson came to mind. I thought about how bringing him in would be a great move on that chessboard. Since our BoxDrop™ model had already reached a high level of success with several hundred locations spanning multiple states, it seemed to me that we could use Jim's logistics and sourcing expertise in that business while also harnessing his chemical and corporate expertise for bioPURE™ if we did indeed buy the company from Brandon. One day I picked up the phone and called Jim to tell him what I was considering and to challenge him. We had a long conversation about the possibilities, during which he told me about the yellow sticky note stuck on the wall behind his desk with his planned exit date written on it. In that moment, I knew for sure that Jim was ready for change. He has a strong mind and phenomenal skills, which he developed throughout a great career, but that fine career was no longer the vehicle for him to reach his full potential. I saw that his life could be altered for the better if he chose to become a Rugged with us. I decided to throw a verbal Chaos Bomb at Jim and told him, "Jim, you can either remain fifty-three going on sixty-five, walking the green line wishing you were playing golf or you can come with us, join the rodeo, enjoy the ride of your life, and feel fifty-three going on thirty-five as a Rugged Entrepreneur."

Jim was set back and a little shocked at first but the chaos in his mind was one intended to awaken his inner Rugged spirit. To our mutual great fortune, Jim took the challenge to allow chaos into his world. He accepted less than half of what he was making at the time and came on the ride based upon my promise that if our company acquired Brandon's company, he would become an owner along with Brandon and my company. I also promised him that if that acquisition didn't work out, we would acquire something else, though I noted that he, like myself and all other Ruggeds, would have to live by the law of the jungle, meaning that as entrepreneurs "we eat what we kill." Put another way, Jim would be taking a 50 percent pay cut in exchange for going on an adventure that would prove to him and others what he was truly capable of once he unleashed his full business potential.

In the interim between that pact and the time we acquired Brandon's business, Jim and I looked at acquiring two other businesses. Jim also did an amazing job sourcing a new product line for BoxDrop™ and projecting the container flow for it. As I am writing this book, Brandon, as bioPURE™'s president and Jim as its CEO, along with some of our stellar team members, have successfully franchised that business. In less than two years, bioPURE™ is at a place that took us almost four years to reach with our BoxDrop™ business and has the potential to be one of the most explosive franchise launches ever. Jim's oldest son, who earned an accounting degree while playing college baseball, and then went to work as the controller of a twenty-million-dollar package manufacturing company, is now the controller of bioPURE™ and is beginning his Rugged Entrepreneur adventure as a 10 percent owner of bioPURE™'s first corporate franchise. Jim and Brandon landed anchor customers such as East Tennessee State University (ETSU), Furman University, and Clemson University, as well as numerous restaurants including some Chic-fil-A franchisees, daycare centers, medical offices, assisted living facilities, and residential households in just the first year of our venture. Jim's younger son, who was just graduating college where he also played baseball, joined us about three months after Jim did. His hope that he would be drafted by a major league ball club did not happen, but luckily for us Kyle became a Rugged, too, and opened a BoxDrop™ location that he and Jim own together. BAM! That business became profitable within his first month. After just eight months, Kyle's BoxDrop™ location was clearing ten to fifteen thousand dollars a month in gross profit, and he was on track to earn a six-figure income as a Rugged Entrepreneur in his early twenties. He was spared going on lots of job interviews after college to find the perfect match. We were that match! Also, there were no more worries for mom and dad. (What parent doesn't worry about their kids' futures?!) Less than two years after Jim decided to come on our Rugged adventure, he woke up and was not only a Rugged himself, he was thriving in three different businesses involving both of his sons and one of his lifelong best friends. Talk about organizing chaos! Jim's life has exploded in the best possible ways, bringing new energy to our organization as well as to his life and business pursuits.

In twenty-seven years of working for the largest business in the area and reaching one of its top positions, Jim was never in the local newspaper. In less than a year and a half of becoming a Rugged, he found himself making the front page in a feature article that also included a picture of his son Tyler demonstrating a bioPURE™ treatment in the East Tennessee State football weight room. It is also very cool for me to watch my son, Aaron, work with Jim and Tyler as part of the bioPURE™ corporate team getting the social media, business operating systems, and advertising models right for bioPURE™ franchising. Aaron and Tyler first met when Jim and I took them to an Atlanta Braves baseball game. They were five years old at the time, and it was their first major league game. It is wonderful to see them building new memories as well as new businesses together.

Organizing Unplanned Chaos

The impact of the 2020 COVID-19 crisis catapulted the bioPURE™ business taking its franchisee applicant list from 23 to over 300 in less than six weeks' time. That crisis alone created the most chaos that I have ever seen in a business, and RSS had two different franchise models operating in two different industries in which to organize chaos. As an entrepreneur you will ultimately face some form of chaos and, if you are not Rugged enough, it can bury you. Our leaders and teams were Rugged enough to organize the COVID-19 chaos and use it to gain market share at an almost unbelievable pace. The bioPURE™ team had a one-week planning meeting wherein a 15-month initial "pioneer" franchise expansion plan was narrowed to just two months. Now, *that's* organizing chaos. The BoxDrop™ team took a week to pivot, modify, and educate a nationwide chain of Rugged Entrepreneurs on operating their business under new protocols in a hurricane of business regulatory changes. Our business team's incredible ability to organize that chaos led to BoxDrop™ growing double digits during the worst three months of the crisis when the industry was down 40 percent and businesses were closing at a record and unheard-of pace. Knowing how to organize that COVID-19 level of chaos was the business equivalent to championship surfing on monster waves. It is exhilarating to control a powerfully and largely uncontrollable force and work your business through it like a master surfer handling a fifty-foot monster wave.

The rewards my wife and I enjoy as a result of accepting the challenge to become Rugged Entrepreneurs who get to play business chess and organize chaos are far greater than the rewards of becoming multi-millionaires have been. Discovering our peak potential has been truly thrilling. We have also seen several others become millionaires. We have helped hundreds create six-figure incomes too. We've found some of our best friends and most trusted advisors through the businesses we own. We've also enticed our own family members and second generations within other families we've already helped to become Rugged Entrepreneurs. These associations have greatly benefited us all. As we build the second half of our life together, it is heartening to know that we will be enjoying our business life with family and dear friends at our side. To enjoy such an inclusive lifestyle is just not possible in any other career. It is also highly unlikely for entrepreneurs who may be financially successful but are not quite Ruggeds.

That, my friend, and hopefully my fellow Rugged, is my best explanation as to why you should develop your complete or critical thinking skills and learn to play business chess very well. It is also why you should learn to organize and even embrace chaos whether it be the kind derived from fast growth, thrown at you in a crisis or created intentionally to help build, change, and challenge people. Chaos is a powerful force and it takes mental toughness, strong critical thinking, and some serious Rugged Sight to use it for great and even market-disrupting breakthroughs. If you learn to create, organize, and utilize a little chaos from time to time, you never know what major force for good it will result in. If you are not already doing these things, you should be. The benefits should be evident from Jim Wilson's and my story. Enlisting a friend in a business chess game and shaking things up a little, is one of the most gratifying adventures I've had. I am only sharing a few of these great stories here, as the many stories I have to tell on this topic could fill a book of its own.

Sometimes while playing business chess and creating and orga-nizing chaos, moves work out far better than you could have imagined. This benefit of being a Rugged is what I call the Law of Reciprocity. As a Rugged you often plant seeds in the lives of others. The seeds come in the form of time, coaching, commitment, being a cheerleader, rewarding success, and investing capital. When those seeds grow into plants and bear fruit, that fruit generates far more seeds than when you first began. It's the universe giving back to you in multiples. If that makes you want to do the same, here is how you do it.

Business Chess 101

First, you must understand the very magic of a chess game and why the more you play the better you become at thinking strategically. In chess, each player has a set of pieces that move differently on the board. Some of those pieces are valued differently than others. The object of the game is to posi-tion your pieces so your opponent's king can no longer move without being taken. (When it is vulnerable, as in just one move from being taken, it is said that your king is in checkmate.) Each player takes turns making a move back and forth capturing the other's pieces and taking both offensive and defensive positions as the game progresses. The strategic thought process in a chess match involves looking at all of your possible moves and anticipating what your opponents' reactions might be. You are also trying to predict what your opponent's overall strategy is based on their move(s). The game usually takes forty or so moves per player before someone is in checkmate. Developing an inner sight for all the possible moves and countermoves—looking two, three, four, or more potential moves into the future—is very challenging. Each layer of forward thought multiplies the ways you might counter your opponent, or they might counter you, so contemplating the moves ahead becomes even more challenging the further out you try to project. Thinking forward in business is similar, but much more complex because there are far more possibilities and far more unpredictable circum-stances in real life than what can arise in a single game of chess.

Scholars generally agree that there are seven phases in the critical thought process. These are taught in preparation for debate. They are as follows:

1. Posing a problem, theory, or question.
2. Gathering data about it.
3. Analyzing the data for its truth, factoring the assumptions and biases that may exist for and against the posed subject.
4. Measuring such assumptions and/or biases found in the data sources.
5. Prioritizing or assigning weight to the different pieces of data you will rely on.
6. Identifying as many possible conclusions as you can, in order to choose those that are best.
7. Communicating the conclusion or conclusions you come to.

Here are some good tips for strengthening your critical thinking process while playing business chess:

- Fully acknowledge that you must develop this skill and that it is important for your business success. Complete or critical thinking helps you evaluate people, options, and circumstances; problem solving; being receptive and responsive to new ideas; processing information, developing deeper levels of understanding; regulating thoughts and reactions' communicating; making good decisions and nimbly acting on them.
- Develop a reading habit that expands your expertise in your industry and your ability to work with people on a broad level.
- Get to know and have frequent conversations with a willing group of advisors in your industry who can answer any questions you may have.

- Set aside a regular time where you can think clearly and search your mind for answers to questions outside of those your research provides. Do not just use research as a crutch. Learn to think on your own feet, relying on your own experiences and observations, as well as on what you have learned from others' experience.
- Look for data from credible experts available online to help you solve specific challenges. Their advice on this platform is abundant and free!
- Concentrate on slowing down. Your brain works rapidly and sometimes gravitates toward an assumption too quickly leading you to see it as fact when it may not be. When you slow down, you can question those assumptions to be certain they are true.
- Use reverse thinking to be sure you have analyzed a situation from multiple angles. Start by exploring how action A causes B; then flip your thinking around and explore if action B actually caused A. It's what Socrates would do!
- When weighing a critical business move, imagine the worst-case scenario (without being too negative) and then question if the effort still produces a good result. Can your team or business withstand that possibility and still make forward progress in the process?
- Keep notes on the issues you have thought through. In the electronic age, maintaining file folders on your business and its issues is easy. The more you write your thoughts out, the more you will be able to commit them to memory. And committing them to memory means they will be easily accessible the next time you are thinking critically about something related to that topic.
- If you have key employees or partners, practice running your thoughts or theories by them several times before addressing a large group. Create what we call "idea talk" wherein you and

they know you are just discussing, debating, and hashing out ideas aloud.

As you start to practice these suggestions, you will find new ways on your own that can help you. Be sure to add your new ideas to this list. Your business and life experiences are different than others and if you start making efforts to improve your critical thinking, you will identify some skills that are unique to you and some you should continue to work on.

Good luck with this process, and if you take it seriously, know that your business chess skills will strengthen and evolve. The better you get at business chess, the stronger your Rugged Sight will become. To complete the development of your Rugged Sight, you will also need to work on communicating your vision in conversations with the people, teams, and organizations you are responsible for leading. Like critical thinking, your ability to communicate thoughts and goals simply and clearly can always be improved upon. The only way to do this is to continually practice. My best time for doing this is during long walks with my wife and our dogs. That time is very conducive to sharing my thoughts with her. If you do this with your spouse or a close friend or confidante, you have to trust and respect whatever opinions they offer and accept their questions and critique with an open mind. This input forces you to answer and explain your ideas well and to possibly alter your presentation or premise completely if their objectivity helps you reconsider your plan. Communicating your Rugged Sight is part of strengthening it because when you communicate it, you solidify it.

I appreciate the very wise old saying, "He who is the greatest teacher is the greatest student." When you teach or communicate something to another person, you develop a deeper sense of your own thoughts on that subject. Learning how to best communicate your Rugged Sight to others strengthens your full business capabilities.

After discussing an idea with my wife, I then do the same with one or more of my trusted advisors. Generally, this is in an attempt to "sell" them on my thought, move, or idea. It is important that you have advisors who have no reason just to agree with you. You must tell them up front that they are free to disagree. You must also treat them with great respect when they raise issues with your presentation or state concerns about specific points. You do not have to go along with their critique, but you must respect it if you want their insight in the future.

In instances where it is very important, write your thoughts out as a story you can then read to yourself. You will find that this exercise helps you commit the data to your memory. The more you commit to memory, the easier it becomes to discuss your thoughts on a moment's notice, either when practicing it or when presenting it to others. This will also help you to learn and develop what I call the Golden Rule of Leadership Communication: If there is something you have to say or there is something you want to be remembered by those hearing it, then speak it from the heart—*not* from your notes. Speaking from the heart or speaking out of passion is almost always more persuasive and engaging for those to whom you are conveying your thoughts Also, buy and read some books on how to be an effective public speaker and take them seriously. In particular, look for books by people who make a living by public speaking. Last, but not least, practice what you learn through your reading as much as you can. Communication skills are priceless.

Rugged Sight, as you recall me saying at the outset of this chapter, involves both the ability to think critically and to communicate the product of those thoughts clearly. It is one of only a few traits that all billionaires I have studied share. That is the very reason why I often call it a "millionaire-to-billionaire skill." Billionaires recognize its importance, and intentionally work on their ability to see as many moves in advance of them happening on the chess board of their company, their industry, and the larger world. They are experts gathering data, processing and analyzing that intel, and envisioning the key moves and countermoves likely to occur down the road. Anyone can work on developing and sharpening that skill, but most entrepreneurs are not as serious or as driven with purpose as self-made billionaires. You can become a million-aire with some average to above-average Rugged Sight, but to become a billionaire, you must train your Rugged Sight to the levels of what is described in chess as a Grand Master.

CHAPTER SEVEN

DRIVE AND PURPOSE

"Some people want it to happen, some people wish it would happen, others make it happen."

—Michael Jordan

I LEARNED A LONG TIME AGO THAT WHEN A LEADER TELLS PEOPLE *what* they should do, it is wise to always explain *why* they should do it and *how* it will impact them. Remember these words: ***"A man convinced against his will is coerced."***

In the preceding pages I have certainly shared a lot of thoughts about *what* you should do and *how* it will likely affect your business, but for a moment I'd like to focus on the *why* of it all. Before we do that, however, I think the following poem written in 1934 by American composer, radio artist, and writer, Dale Wimbrow, will put you in the right mind frame for that discussion.

The Guy in the Glass

When you get what you want in your struggle for pelf,
And the world makes you King for a day,
Then go to the mirror and look at yourself,
And see what that guy has to say.

For it isn't your Father, or Mother, or Wife
Who judgment upon you must pass.
The feller whose verdict counts most in your life,
Is the guy staring back from the glass.

He's the feller to please, never mind all the rest,
For he's with you clear up to the end,
And you've passed your most dangerous difficult test,
If the guy in the glass is your friend.

You may be like Jack Horner and "chisel" a plum,
And think you're a wonderful guy,
But the man in the glass says you're only a bum,
If you can't look him straight in the eye.

You can fool the whole world down the pathway of years,
And get pats on the back as you pass,
But your final reward will be heartache and tears,
If you've cheated the guy in the glass.

—DALE WIMBROW ©1934

Now that you've read this poem, I want you literally to go to a mirror, look at your reflection, and knowing that it is just you and yourself before that mirror, I want you to get *honest* with that self. I mean, *deeply* honest. Think of nothing else.

Now, with all the truthfulness you can muster between you and yourself, answer these two questions: *"What do I want?" and "What are things that drive me?"*

If you are wondering why you are doing this or why you need to dig so deep to truthfully answer what should be simple questions, I have a simple explanation. In all of my years of studying leadership, history, entrepreneurialism, capitalism, and having the opportunity to lead and coach others, build teams, and build entire organizations, I have found that one common factor preventing people from building and harnessing drive and purpose is their lack of honesty with themselves. Highly successful Ruggeds learn to be blatantly honest with their reflection in the mirror. They learn not to let frivolous distractions and social pressures throw them off the path of what they really want. You cannot fool yourself if you want to be a Rugged. People who aren't truthful with themselves about what drives them, rarely achieve what they are capable of. They may even follow paths others set for them. That is no way to be a leading force in the way that a disruptor is.

Societal norms and the way people are raised and educated have continuously pressured many, at least outwardly, to pursue careers that fit the confining world view of those who appear to be judging them. In any group, you will always find people with critical or disapproving tendencies, but you cannot afford to be entrapped by their snares or you will never build true drive and purpose. You must accept the fact that it is okay to have personal wants and needs. It is okay to desire things—and by *things*, I mean skills, influence, challenge, wisdom, notoriety, power, material possessions, spiritual awareness, good health, the ability to help or empower others, the ability to lead people, the ability to lead organizations, you name it. It is okay to think about doing something great or *big* in a world that is otherwise designed to hold you back from achieving anything beyond what the majority achieves. It is okay to be driven by a competitive urge or the desire to succeed. It's okay to want to leave a legacy behind. Since most people are not entrepreneurs, they don't like the light that a hardworking, success-minded, competitive Rugged Entrepreneur shines on them. The world is quick to point out the flaws in anyone who desires more in life or who will not be constrained or overly influenced by others' judgments of them. Remember, most people *choose* to perform at an average level. Is it any wonder that they push against those who boldly choose to be different—against those who set the expectation bar higher by working harder to build something far beyond what already exists?

Honestly knowing and embracing both what you want and what excites you in the short- and long-term without being encumbered mentally by societal pressure, is essential to building drive and purpose and unleashing your full potential.

Can you break that societal pressure? Can you say what it is that you want candidly and plainly, without dressing it up to sound lofty, altruistic, or like you are somehow bettering all of mankind? Mushy mission and purpose statements are a dime a dozen and are often created just to try to disguise ambition in a way that makes it more acceptable to the outside world. There is nothing wrong with lofty ideals or altruistic missions, but there is also nothing wrong with having simple, immediate, and clear goals, especially if those simply stated goals lead you to what you want and are likely the best path leading you to finding purpose.

"Drive," as a noun and in the psychological sense of the word, is defined as, "The strong force or forces of determination that move one to do or achieve something." Drivers (the things that drive someone) can be many, so when we use the words, "drive" and "drivers," we are referring to plural motivations.

Purpose is the reason why a person or organization exists. We speak of it in the singular, but, of course, you can have more than one purpose. You can have a purpose for a business. You can have multiple businesses each with its own purpose. You can also have purpose separate from your businesses. And sometimes you can operate a business on drive alone, as many people do initially, without having identified that larger super purpose we most associate with the word. Purpose can come before drive but that is rare, and not usually the fastest way to get started. Drive will generally get you going a lot faster than identifying purpose, which might take years.

Can you get deeply honest with yourself about what you want or what will drive you *now*, as in over the next three to six months? How about over the next one to three years? If so, drive is enough to get you started; you will find purpose in the journey. Down the road, as in over the next five to ten years and even longer, you will define some life achievements that you will want to accomplish. That is where you will find purpose. If you do not answer these questions openly now (and again at different intervals in your growth), building real drive, and ultimately finding and fulfilling purpose, is almost impossible.

To work on getting honest with yourself, let's look to the example of two handmade Bugatti sports cars that are creations of power and beauty—the Veyron Super Sport and the Chiron. Beyond being works of incredible craftsmanship, beauty, and design, both of these amazing vehicles were built to set records in speed, and they did, reaching 270 to 304 mph. The Veyron has a 16 cylinder 64-valve quad turbocharged engine that produces 1200 horsepower and goes from zero to one hundred miles per hour in just 2.5 seconds. You can bet that its engine loves some high-octane fuel. In fact, it has a 26½-gallon fuel tank to make sure the driver can feed the engine. Your own drive works the same way. Knowing what you honestly want is the high-octane fuel you and your business engine need to achieve speed, momentum, and success. Having that vital piece of information means that you can take off at 304 miles per hour toward your destiny in no time at all!

As we have described, drive and purpose are not the same things. *Drive* is the fuel that feeds you as a Rugged so that you can do all the mental and physical work required to move people, projects, and events forward. *Purpose*, for a Rugged, is the tank that holds the fuel safely so it can be fed into the engine. One of the advantages you have over a

Bugatti is that you can actually have more than one tank. You can have tanks for each business or organization that you work with. You can separate personal tanks from business tanks based on what you believe is right for your life. And you can install bigger tanks as the need or your purpose expands. Once you understand and embrace this concept, you will have reached a milestone in your Rugged journey.

It may seem a little backward to start with the fuel instead of the tank, but it is what you must do because purpose isn't always something you know how to identify at first. You may have *goals* and a *mission*, but that is not *purpose*, per se. I have seen people lost for years. They have searched to *find* their purpose before trying their hand at any substantial work or before getting tangible results. Even without purpose, you can use drive to fuel your engine and get things moving forward until you finally see the larger purpose in what you are doing. For most entrepreneurs, just earning a good living provides fuel and gives them the drive to progress with or without purpose. So always identify what drives you personally, even in the absence of purpose. The purpose will follow, I assure you.

There are many common drivers. I offer a few examples with the following. Feel free to use them at your discretion, as not all of them will drive you the same way that they drive me, nor do they have to. Also be aware that what drives you may not necessarily drive your partners, employees, service providers, or customers. Pay attention to their drivers anyway—they are very important in team building and creating customer and employee satisfaction. That said, there is often more common ground than you may realize.

Many of the self-made millionaires and billionaires I have been blessed to meet and/or study were driven initially by the simple desire to escape poverty or to get to a place where they could find opportunity. They didn't have time to identify any sense of grand purpose before getting to work. Many had to escape a country or atmosphere where little to no social or economic advancement existed. Just getting to a place where they could seek those advantages in the form of a job or education provided their fuel.

In my studies, data has generally shown that foreigners who come to America are seven to eleven times more likely to become millionaires than native-born Americans. To me, the reason is just plain common sense. A large percentage of those foreigners come to the United States with the singular and resolute drive to put themselves in an environment where they can create a better opportunity. By opportunity, I mean the chance to do what Americans before them did: find a starting point and work their way up from there. It is called "climbing the ladder" to success. Too many Americans today expect to start somewhere between the middle and the upper-middle levels. They lack the drive to start at the so-called "bottom" and work their way up, amassing useful knowledge at every step along the way. Sadly, America spoils its youth so much that there are tens of thousands of twenty- and thirty-somethings still living with mommy and daddy. There are even forty-year-old adults who still lack drive because they failed to identify what they wanted or what drove them at an earlier age. They were taught to "pursue their passion" or "find their purpose." Too bad they weren't taught to start at the best and most opportunistic "bottom rung" and figure out what would drive their ascent to the top from there.

I do not want this to be some general condemnation of all our youth in their late teens, twenties, and even thirties. We still have amazing young athletes, special forces soldiers, and successful Rugged Entrepreneurs who are driven—and many of them are better equipped to do more now than those generationally older were at their same age. It is a fact, however, that U.S. multigenerational household living has been on a dramatic rise in the last thirty-five years. Pew Research shows that the number of Americans living in multi-generationally mixed households nearly doubled from just 12 percent in 1980 to 20 percent by 2016. I blame much of this on two generations of children having been raised on a "seek your passion, chase what moves you, find your purpose" philosophy, rather than being raised on the expectation that you jump into meaningful work and make something more of it as you go. Up to and into the early 1980s, young people were taught to seek work that aligned with their skills, start where they could, and rise to the top accordingly, being fortunate for the opportunity and proud of their ability to gain independence and success.

Until you identify and embrace what drives you and cultivate an intentional process to add to that list of drivers, it is highly unlikely that you will identify any grand sense of purpose. When you pinpoint your drivers, they give you fuel to finish projects and to look for new and better ones. You will notice that as you climb one ladder of opportunity, new ones appear that will often take you higher and increase your possibilities. This upward spiral creates more confidence, greater insight, and enables you to see even more opportunities. If you are always waiting for that perfect ladder, with a banner that reads "My Purpose in Life" swaying from it, you will likely find yourself stuck on the ground for a very long time. If you haven't found your purpose yet, don't worry about it, no matter what generation you are in. Most Ruggeds start with Drive and discover their Purpose well into their journey. Your purpose will become clearer along the way too.

To identify the fuel you need now, you should return to the questions I posed earlier: "What do you want?" and "What drives you?" Any number of things big and small can drive you, and the more specific you are identifying them, the better the quality your fuel will be.

One of the things that drove me when I was a younger entrepreneur, and still drives me today, is *credibility*. It is important to me that people think of me as a hard worker who gets results and as someone who builds credibility into the teams and organizations that I lead. It enables other industry leaders and the competition to trust that we are an organization that makes an impact. Having that *street cred* is like having extra people advertise your business for you. I imagine that desire for credibility came in part because, as a young entrepreneur, I frequently had to prove my capability to much more senior and experienced people. I also had to find ways to lead people who were older than me. Credibility was critical in doing that.

When we build mastermind teams in our organizations, we do so selectively. This selectiveness makes the credibility of those chosen known to the team and the world in which it operates. We know how to promote the people we choose so that their qualifications and credibility are broadcast inside of our company and within the larger industry too. Does your leadership team know how to acknowledge one another and build organizational credibility? Do you recognize your people's contributions in meetings? Do you invite your leadership team or teams to travel to conventions, shows, vendor meetings, and other such public forums so that you can acknowledge them (and they, one another) in the presence of the industry? Do you do things that make your team members and their credibility known within your field? Organizational credibility is a driver within the company, too, because many people (whether they will admit it or not), are driven by being acknowledged or by being part of special teams. It empowers them with a sense of pride.

A Rugged learns that credibility is critical for success in business and they make earning it a priority. You can always increase credibility in an area where you have already earned it. And you can earn it in areas you are just beginning to explore. Credibility is the only driver I believe *all* Ruggeds must create. There are numerous other drivers such as money or material reward, recognition, influence, power, protection against loss, helping others, being the best, the fastest, the most innovative and/ or the most disruptive, creating and building something, having passion or pride in an achievement ... the list goes on and on. You must honestly identify the things that will drive you personally (the longer the list, the better) but having credibility must be one of them.

I mentioned money, and that is definitely another popular driver. I have never met a successful entrepreneur who, at one point or another, wasn't financially motivated. Before you allow the world's judgment to affect you on this point, take a good look at Mother Teresa who was canonized as a saint in September of 2016. Mother Teresa is famous for her inspirational love. She earned her sainthood living and teaching that example with so much credibility. Even so, Mother Teresa also knew that raising money was crucial in order to help impoverished people in India.

She boldly set up one-on-one and group meetings with world leaders to raise the money needed to pay for medicine, doctors, food, resources, and even buildings. From a Rugged Entrepreneurial perspective, her efforts were the equivalent of sales pitches and each of those pitches stressed the absolute importance of capital and accessing it. Without profitable individuals and businesses generating money, there would not have been any capital for Mother Teresa's work. Being a successful Rugged Entrepreneur and building your skyscraper of a business will automatically create ripples of financial success and opportunity for you to help others too. Knowing that the totality of what you're building will be of great benefit to the world someday should help you ignore others' judgmental eyes as you are building it.

More often than not, the initial drive for a Rugged is just what it was for my father: the desire to get off of a dirt road and out of a frame-only house with no indoor plumbing, insulation, or air conditioning. The will to escape impoverishment and all of its constraints can often be a much greater driver than any immediate singular material want. Once my father achieved that goal, he continued to set his earning bench-marks higher each year, providing more for his family until his ambitions broadened beyond just lifestyle and monetary goals. I have seen, studied, and coached numerous others who continuously set higher and higher annual earnings objectives just as he did.

Very early in my career, I had a goal to earn $100,000 in a single year solely from my ownership interests in two companies, one of which I owned and ran outright, and the other of which I was a partial owner and responsible for day-to-day operations. Just like my father, I believed that targeted income would provide a very good home and lifestyle for my family. As I have already said in this book, all Ruggeds face at least one time when they have to eat what they kill. The drive to survive financially is one of a Rugged's most defining skills and having done it successfully is something they all take great personal pride in.

When that $100,000 goal was achieved, the major material thing I wanted was not just to own a home, but to custom-build one from the ground up. I wanted it specially designed for our family and how we wished to use it. I was right about $100,000 being enough to buy a home where we could live comfortably, but I had to reset the bar higher to be able to afford all of the other things we would need week in and week out. My wife and I got deeply honest about what we wanted, and we decided that we still wished for a custom home. That required us to raise the financial bar to $250,000. We spent $4,000 to have custom plans drawn for the house of our dreams. I kept a set of those plans behind my desk and looked at them almost every Friday. I told people about the house, showed some the plans, and promised my wife we would build it once that income goal was reached. We talked about how we would decorate it and what it would be like to use it for entertaining friends and family. We even spent time looking for the perfect lot to build it on and began making a list of lots we liked as we found them.

Knowing that credibility was a driver for me, I knew how to set myself up with my mouth to either lose or gain credibility on the subject. Remember, I said you have to *build* drive, and you do that by figuring out what you want and what drives you. In the case of the house, what my wife and I wanted was to be able to custom-build the perfect home for raising our family. What drove me was not losing credibility with her and the others I told about it. I call that "throwing the football."

When I was a young boy playing youth football, my dad would some-times take me to the high school games where they would throw out plastic mini footballs to the fans at halftime. On many days after school with little else to do (there were no cellphones or video games then), I would go out in our back yard and play both sides of an imaginary game with that little football. I would pretend I was Joe Montana, the quarterback of the San Francisco 49ers, throwing the ball to wide receiver Jerry Rice. I would also pretend to be the announcer offering play-by-play coverage. First, I'd describe myself as the QB scrambling to throw a pass; then I'd describe myself as the receiver reaching out to catch the pass. Every time I caught the ball, I would try to throw the next pass a little farther, making myself have to stretch even more. My hope was to make that perfect long-dive catch. I would dig out an imaginary end zone line with my heel and use it as a goal line. That way, as each pass got longer, I got closer to stretching my arms out over that goal line and making a fantasy crowd-pleasing catch for a touchdown.

Once I learned in real life that having credibility, and not losing it, were essential drivers in my success, I intentionally set myself up to achieve whatever I wanted to by verbally throwing out the football, just as I had done in my childhood game. I created ways to express that "business pass" to as many people as I could without seeming too arrogant, obnoxious, or ridiculous. I purposefully set myself up for either living up to what I told people I would do (catching the football) or not living up to it (dropping the ball). Creating those business passes/credibility drivers for myself has always been one of my greatest strengths. Be aware, however: you will not always catch the ball. In those instances, you will have to accept personal responsibility for the miss. Knowing that I would have to accept such responsibility and that I'd also have to explain my failure have always made me work extremely hard on catching that ball.

Over time, I learned that as long as people could see that I worked diligently to be able to "catch the ball," the amount of lost credibility if I failed was not as great as I had feared it would be because people respected the effort to reach for it. I also learned that when you own up to not catching the ball, you earn a different type of credibility—one that makes you relatable as a human and that makes the people you lead more comfortable about throwing the ball out and stretching themselves too.

The organizations, people, and teams I led began taking pride in both throwing and catching the ball. This was doubly effective when I learned how to incorporate their goals, interests, and own personal drivers into the description of the business advancement I was asking the team to make. They also knew that if they caught the ball, I would happily give them credit for it.

When we finally reached the $250,000 goal two years later, we hired a contractor and had the house built exactly to plan. It felt so good to know we caught that ball and earned the touchdown.

Setting a new round of goals after that was important. I was starting yet another business and decided that I needed a personal reward to drive me to build its sales volume quickly. I remembered a college friend who had been given his father's Rolex before he went off to school. It seemed like such a classic yet rugged watch. I didn't envy him or covet that watch, but I did think that it was very powerful that his father had given this heirloom to him at such a pivotal time in his life. That neat image had always stuck with me but buying a watch that cost several thousand dollars had been outside of my comfort zone. I wasn't much of a watch person at the time and had never even worn one, but once I started to be honest and open with myself about what kind of personal things would drive me to meet this larger goal I had, that Rolex came to mind. I decided that when the new business generated a net income equal to three times the cost of the watch, I would treat myself to one.

To be sure I would reach my goal, I also set some competitive sales volume levels for the new company. A few established competitors known for their fast growth had reached these sales levels before, so I knew they were attainable yet still a reach for such a young company. I got to know the story behind those competitive businesses and how long it took them to hit certain milestones before deciding that our new company would hit them in less time than they had. I then threw that football out to everyone we were working with, telling them we would be a disruptor in the marketplace and would set a new pace for what is defined as fast growth if we accomplished this goal better and faster than all the other companies did before us. In addition to my own personal reward of getting the Rolex, I set up some creative compensation rewards for the key people on the team as well as for all the others who would be working toward meeting this goal. Rewarding others and having a team is why the profit amount had to be three times that of the watch. Teams get more done, and they get it done faster.

In this example, what I wanted was a Rolex. What drove me was getting that watch, beating some of our competitor's timelines, and earning street credibility in the process. Once again throwing out the football by stating that we would outperform our fastest competitors helped set us up for accomplishing our goal. This endeavor gave me the opportunity to show that I could exercise the discipline and skill of *delayed gratification*. I loved to coach this skill and wanted a way to prove that I personally exercise it. It was necessary to credibly evidence that my skill in this area was current. I had already reached an income level to easily afford the watch and anyone with eyes to see knew it. This was to demonstrate to those I was coaching that I could delay my gratification or satisfaction for something I wanted until my difficult goal was reached, despite easily being able to afford it. If I had not achieved the goal, the reward would not be attained either.

Delayed gratification is a useful skill to have and not only brings significant rewards, but also generates a healthy respect for you among the people you lead. If you want or expect others to exhibit something, it is a good idea to have exhibited it first yourself. Modeling a skill makes it easy for others to follow. Of course, that is not *always* the case. For instance, someone who has never dunked a basketball can still be a great basketball coach. That said, having the credibility of doing something often makes teaching it easier. It took me a little over two years to reach the Rolex goal, but when it was hit, I bought the watch and continue to wear it to this day as a reminder that delayed gratification is important, and that knowing what I want and that it can be achieved is also important.

I realize that some people reading this are already judging me and asking, *What about charity? What about helping others? What about curing disease?* Being honest with and allowing myself to have those basic material wants and identifying drivers that would also push me to attain them also opened me up to learning so much about Drive and Purpose. When you realize how something works on you and others, it naturally becomes a skill that you can grow.

This may not be the case for you, but for me it was only after I reached a comfort level with my ability to provide for my family financially that I could really start to develop purpose in my business and life. For most people, it is very difficult to focus on a "greater" sense of purpose when they are struggling just to make a decent living. Being honest with myself about what my drivers were while building businesses and generating income helped me arrive at a level where my mind was broader, more confidant, and more open to having purpose. For me, the ability to build a business around Purpose was something I was only able to envision and do after I had gained enough other experience. That experience led me to discover what I loved and was passionate about beyond just being financially independent.

I truly believe that allowing myself to be driven by my basic wants, enabled me to create more important drivers and ultimately purpose. Those early goals led to a level of financial success that has empowered us to be charitable in ways and to degrees we never could have dreamt of. I might have spent years being charitable, but without truly being driven, I would likely only be charitable on a very minimal scale today. When people are in charitable need, it is true that they often benefit from love, time, and compassion. That said, it is often far more powerful to be able to provide monetary solutions that address a great number of people's needs at once. Had I not learned how to honestly drive myself, I never would have become the financial provider I am, and we never would have become the far more charitable financial givers we are now.

By far, my greatest driver came after I was asked to make the choice to continue running and possibly someday own the entire beverage wholesale business in which I was a 30 percent owner or to continue to build my two smaller companies. Daff and I had a comfortable six-figure income and a nice lifestyle at the time. We were well past the point of having to eat what we kill, and our plans for the future looked favorable. Two-thirds of our income came from that beverage wholesale job, so leaving it was a big choice to have to make. Yes, I was forced to choose but the choice was mine to make. I chose going my own way and that decision led to a two-year stretch during which my father and I did not speak a single word to each other as he was the 70 percent owner of that beverage wholesale company and also the person who told me that I had to determine my path one way or the other.

Yes, my choice put Daff and me in a place where we had to downsize and survive off what we could scratch together, but more importantly, it made me come to what remains my most powerful driving thought to date. It is easy to say *live with no regrets*, but in this circumstance, I had to live with the concern that if I did not build a business as big or bigger in opportunity or economic scale as that wholesale beverage business, I would forever be sorry about what my choice had done to my family financially. It was a thought that drove me every day and it was one I never had to speak out loud. The enormity of that reality was evident to all who knew me.

I realized that by being asked to make that choice, I had not earned my father's full respect. And why should I have had his full respect when I hadn't started from scratch in the entrepreneurial world and learned how to survive by eating what I killed as he had done? Yes, I had succeeded in the job. Yes, I had grown the business by adding a number of successful soft drink lines to the distributorship. Yes, I had been elected to advisory and state boards in the industry. And yes, I had started other businesses. But I had not done as much as what he did, nor had I survived the excruciating downturns and chaos he had.

From that experience, I was driven to earn my father's respect and that led to my becoming driven to always earn and maintain credibility, as already discussed. You see, I gave my 30 percent of the stock in my father's company back to him and walked away with a vehicle and the forgiveness of a $100,000 loan that I had taken from the company to build that dream house, which we then had to sell. The stock was worth millions, but in my heart, I knew it was my father's company. The stock was given to me when he retired from running it. Offering me the opportunity to handle the company at such a young age and the chance to likely become its sole owner one day was an honor he was bestowing upon me as his only son. When I chose to go out on my own, I could not, with any dignity, have kept that stock even though it was mine to keep and no one could take it from me, nor did my father demand that I give it back.

Sometimes the toughest choices we make and the ones that cause us the greatest challenges, can also be the ones that create the greatest opportunities for something incredible to follow. How will you perceive and face your toughest challenges?

I hope you can create honest and simple drivers for yourself because from that starting point you will be able to build so much, and you will also discover deeper drivers to take you further on the journey. Your drivers may not be as emotional to you as mine were to me. Not speaking to my father, who had always been one of my heroes, was as affecting as you might imagine. Or your drivers may actually be more emotional or more serious in nature. Your journey and discoveries will be unique to you. They are yours to traverse in your own way. What I can say from experience is that bridges between broken relationships can be re-constructed and mutual respect can be earned. Today my father not only remains one of my heroes, he is on the board of our largest business, on multiple advisory boards for several other businesses we own, and he and I are EQUAL partners in a holdings company that includes a large construction and land development business. As I have said before, he is one of my most trusted advisors. I speak to him weekly, and I meet face to face with him at least once a month. Most important to me is that I was able to earn his respect, and because of that we are now much more than just father and son; we are really good friends and business partners. In every adversity a Rugged is able to find an equal or greater opportunity to be driven forward. Discovering what truly drives you will bring about rewards that are far greater than you could ever expect and way beyond material reward.

Now let's shift from Drive to Purpose for a moment. For us, Purpose is very serious and should never be thrown out to simply motivate people because it sounds good or because it can manipulate others into doing something you want them to do after you start working with them. We have seen numerous businesses create those type of self-serving mission statements, doling them out cheaply. If you do not mean it from your heart or you simply wear it on your shirtsleeve for all the public to see, you will set yourself up for failure or, at the very least, you will fall short of what you are truly capable of achieving. Purpose is usually something discovered with time and experience as you work your way through challenging situations. It is not something you generally write down early in life and hope to live up to later. A quote that is often attributed to Abraham Lincoln states: ***"You can fool all the people some of the time and some of the people all the time, but you cannot fool all the people all the time."*** Attempting to fool others with some lofty, but not all together truthful, statement of purpose will not lead you to building the complete success you are capable of. Even though you may be able to fool some, you darn sure will not be able to fool *the guy in the glass.*

As my wife and I started having success in multiple businesses and we reached an income where our financial desires were more than being met, we found ourselves gravitating towards the things we liked most about some businesses and away from what we didn't like about others.

During one of our long walks, Daphene and I talked about what we wanted the larger purpose of our business life to be. We pondered the legacy of that part of our life. We also talked about our passion for American capitalism and the lack of its credible and passionate teaching in our educational system. We talked about the people we saw as hypocrites for promoting less than truthful missions while building their businesses, and our disdain for such hypocrisy. We discussed seeing so many people and businesses willing to be less than honest when stating and promoting a purpose because they could hide behind that purpose or use it like smoke and mirrors to create the illusion of success. We knew we had to be different. If we identified a purpose, it had to be something that we could really live up to. There had to be visible results from advancing that purpose.

After several more walks and after analyzing our current mix of businesses, we concluded that one day we would build a business whose mission was purely to help others understand capitalism and free enterprise, and to empower our clients to become successful entrepreneurs who identified themselves in that same light. We had already worked with and studied some people who advertised that as their purpose but who helped very few people reach any financial independence. We had seen enough self-aggrandizing false prophets. These were people who were more preoccupied with their own importance than they were with effectively helping others. We knew that a business run by us with the purpose of empowering others to become what we call Rugged Entrepreneurs, had to bear the fruit of actually helping large numbers of people become financially independent in their own business.

Numerous organizations claim to have a purpose. If they really mean it, the fruit of their labor should be evident on their tree. Everyone should be able to see how much of it they actually helped to grow. One of the most important lessons I have learned while studying others is what *not* to do or how *not* to treat people if you truly wish to empower them. Purpose is not just what drives you. It is what you exist for and what enables you to feel great about the outcome of the work you are driven to do. Purpose enables you to feel a healthy pride because you identified the fuel (the things that drive you) and you put that fuel in your "purpose" tank to help you reach your goal.

Once we stated our purpose to ourselves, which was to *empower entrepreneurs,* we looked to see if that purpose was part of every business we owned. We began divesting ourselves of any interests that didn't help us fulfill that purpose or didn't bear fruit in a measurable way. Then we began focusing on those that did. Once you identify a true purpose, it literally possesses you. It haunts your mind whenever you are not doing something that helps advance that very purpose. Mark Twain is well known for his witty quotes and one of my favorites from him is this, **"The two most important days in your life are the day you are born and they day you find out why."**

Empowering Entrepreneurs was a purpose, which grew organically from our years of experiences and included teaching entrepreneurs or would-be entrepreneurs about such topics as capitalism, self-reliance, free enterprise, leadership, team building, personal accountability, financial responsibility, American entrepreneurial history, mental toughness, business chess, organizing chaos, deservance, and all of the other skills and traits we could think of that a successful business owner might need to know. It enveloped our passion for history, specifically what has driven people to create entrepreneurial success on a high level in the past. There were so many subjects to cover in the mission of Empowering Entrepreneurs, that it would have been easy to build measurements into the program that fooled us and others into thinking we helped more people than we did. So we set only one truly relevant measurement: **How many people and how diverse a group of people, have become financially independent as entrepreneurs due to what we did to help empower them in that endeavor?**

The singular most important reflection of our seriousness about building purpose into our business and into our lives was how many entrepreneurs we could see and be engaged with who then created financial independence with the guidance we and our organizations provided.

It is an easy number to measure when you are engaged directly with the owners, and one that you cannot hide from. In the business world of consultants, commission sales, business-opportunity sellers, multilevel marketing companies, franchise businesses, licensing opportunities, and numerous others, there are countless false prophets who claim to have a mission of helping others succeed financially when they know full well that the percentage of those they engage with who actually become financially independent through their empowerment program is often less than a paltry 1 or 2 percent. The world of revolving door empowerment models, programs, and consultants is replete with hucksters who have an extremely small number of success stories to show for their work. Their business model is generally one that fools the masses and only feeds the upper echelon of their organizations.

Knowing that the world was full of such business empowerment hucksters, we placed our intense focus on being customer obsessed. Our sole purpose was and still is to build companies that truly empower entrepreneurs (our customers). The success of that empowerment had to be measured by the entrepreneur's ability to achieve financial success *and* independence for themselves.

In addition to empowering entrepreneurs who had an existing business, or even just a business idea, we knew we also wanted to empower those who had an entrepreneurial spirit but had not yet decided on a specific business to pursue. One of the ways to do this was by building licensing, franchising, and educational opportunities that those clients or students could participate in. Franchising which is considered a higher level of systemized business ownership than licensing or other business ownership possibilities that do not qualify as franchises, generally have an annual attrition rate of about 10 to 13 percent. This is in a world where studies show that 20 to 30 percent of small businesses fail in their first year, and 50 percent of business startups fail in their first five years. The lower failure rate (thus the higher credibility of franchises) generally comes from being able to measure and evidence that the systemized business works. We knew that *anything* we worked on should have the goal of producing a better rate of success and lower rate of attrition than the general franchise industry.

As we began to pursue our passion, we created more and more ideas and investigated more and more possible opportunities. Some of them worked and others didn't. We either adjusted and made those that weren't working work, or we dropped them all together. We started businesses from scratch, bought existing businesses, merged entities through legal transactions, and constantly worked on building mastermind teams to improve those businesses. In that process, we created our own classifications of entrepreneurs, defining which types were best suited for different kinds of businesses. Those classifications include Rugged, corporate, and professional entrepreneurs as we discussed previously. In building the constructs of the Rugged Holdings umbrella, we were able to add new features to our existing businesses to help empower them even more than before. Soon we created the concept of Rugged University and our Rugged-based consulting services company as well as Rugged ETV and The Rugged Nation Network. Opportunities to create credible entrepreneurial educational experiences for students at universities such as ETSU evolved through our working business laboratory, Rugged Buc Labs, and our mission clarified even more. As our entrepreneurial empowering businesses continued to boom and our focused ideas began to materialize, so too did the results of our purpose.

In my fifty-plus years of life, some thirty-five to forty years have been spent in entrepreneurial thought and/or experience. During that time, Daff and I made hundreds of friends and contacts inside and outside our family, social, and business lives. We have fallen in love with the concept of collaboration, especially with high level entrepreneurial and business thinkers, on whom we often shine a spotlight, discuss business, and solve challenges with. We have reached a place where our primary business interests are all about one of four things: empowering entrepreneurs, promoting and educating others on capitalism and entrepreneurship, holding real estate, and being in business with family and friends with whom we truly want to spend our second half of life. We have also become multimillionaires, far surpassing any annual financial goals we ever dreamed possible.

As we enter what we think of as the autumn of our business life, we've begun refining our purpose even further. By now we have certainly proven that we are committed to the purposes of promoting and teaching entrepreneurialism, Rugged Entrepreneurialism, and the advancement of free enterprise. We have helped hundreds of people become financially independent. All of our businesses empower entrepreneurs and are well established with great leaders, who, along with us, continue to grow that mission. We have been a part of multi-generational entrepreneurial success in multiple businesses and with numerous families. We have spread entrepreneurialism to strangers, friends, and family as well as through all but one of the fifty states and into several other countries. These businesses generate financial independence, charitable contributions to numerous causes, make a great tax contribution to America's society, and they help provide jobs to thousands who support all of our great Rugged Entrepreneurs in the chain of manufacturing, supply, and retail channeling. In living out that purpose, we set in motion a movement of empowerment and Rugged Entrepreneurial energy that will far outlast our breathing days, and we *love* watching it grow.

In this amended version of our purpose, we have chosen to create an adjunct entrepreneurial group of collaborative friends for whom we have a mutual respect and with whom we truly enjoy spending a lot of time, both socially and in business. We have similar ideals and principals and look to make our achievements fun and fulfilling in ways that benefit others but allow us to enjoy a day-to-day lifestyle where we are able to have more fun with each other and our families than our previous schedules allowed. We live and work simultaneously in great balance. We are intentionally cultivating what we call "second-generation leaders" in all of our various businesses and are also deliberately building our personal experiences. Creating a relationship-centric business group that enjoys life together is exciting and gives us reasons to be creative in ways we never thought of before.

We see building this ultimate team of family and friends who are connected through multiple businesses as a win-win for everyone. This collaboration between owners produces increased financial success while also fostering a lifestyle enriched with lots more mobility and flexibility. Working with friends this way allows us to blend business with pleasure and enjoy a whole life experience. We can also create multi-generational success, all while focusing on the business purpose of empowering entrepreneurs. By multi-generational, I don't only mean that we work with the second or third generations of families (something we love to do), but I mean that we also work with second and third generations of leadership and mastermind people inside our business adventures. We want whatever we've built and whatever we continue to build to last and dynamically change lives for a very long time.

This final and personal Purpose involves introducing our closest and most talented life friends and family to what you have seen me call the "Rodeo." We are literally lassoing loved ones and their grown children into an environment that is wildly powerful and offers immense opportunity. It is such a crazy and fun way to live and work, we want them to experience it too! We've asked these loved ones a set or type of probing questions that you are already familiar with if you've read this far: *"Are you fifty-something going on sixty-five, just walking the green line until retirement? Or are you fifty-something going on thirty-five with enough daring wisdom and life experience to take the ride of your life?"* The Rodeo to us is a business and personal lifestyle that combines our shared passion for promoting entrepreneurialism and empowering entrepreneurs with our love of spending fun-filled days with close friends and family. As we look for and see the best in accomplished people, we invite them to join us. Their participation makes the Rodeo better and also offers them a shot at a better quality of life—one with more zest, more purpose, and likely more success.

This last and somewhat selfish purpose for Daff and me has led us to doing business with some of our oldest friends, including one whom I've known since preschool, and several whom I have known since high school and college, as well as immediate family members on both my and Daff's side of the family. The Rodeo gang ranges from the likes of my father to one of my favorite drinking buddies and a whole list of old and new friends who have joined to become collaborative leaders in our various organizations. The rewards, beyond the monetary ones, have been many. Working this way has been exhilarating and has even served as a kind of fountain of youth.

Never before has it been so easy to blend business and life in one grand adventure. Digital communication speeds our ability to grow faster and faster and air travel's increasing affordability has enabled us to participate in the Rodeo from wherever we are. Simply stated: the evolved purpose of the Rodeo is to continue to empower entrepreneurs in the company of life friends. Who knows what other forms of purpose and businesses we will create together as a group. What we do know is that we will be doing as much of it as possible on our own terms. We will be there to uplift each other, collaborate with each other, hold each other accountable, cry with each other, laugh with each other, raise our kids and grandkids together, travel, and enjoy the success of others together. We will also manifest business models and business break-throughs together, be disruptive together, and flat out fill our second half of life with building skyscrapers together. In many ways, we believe our example can influence the way everyone creates work-life balance, but particularly the way those in the autumn of their careers do so.

You, my friend, and hopefully by now, fellow Rugged, will have to build your own skyscraper. You have all of the God-given tools you need to do it and then some more from the pages of this book. It will not be easy, nor will it always be simple. There will be many failures on the way to achieving success and many learning experiences on the way to discovering purpose. I can tell you one thing for certain; it will be RUGGED and that will make it your unique story to share one day in your book about a life even better than mine if you want it to be. Travel well on your Rugged path, but before we part, I will leave you with this one final poem and challenge.

The poem is by Will Allen Dromgoole and reads as follows:

The Bridge Builder
—WILL ALLEN DROMGOOLE

An old man going a lone highway
Came at the evening, cold and gray,
To a chasm, vast, and deep and wide,
Through which was flowing a sullen tide.

The old man crossed in the twilight dim;
The sullen stream had no fear for him;
But he turned, when safe on the other side,
And built a bridge to span the tide.

"Old man," said a fellow pilgrim, near,
"You are wasting strength with building here;
Your journey will end with the ending day;
You never again will pass this way;
You've crossed the chasm, deep and wide-
Why build you this bridge at the evening tide?"

The builder lifted his old gray head:
"Good friend, in the path I have come," he said,
"There followeth after me today,
A youth, whose feet must pass this way.

> *This chasm, that has been naught to me,*
> *To that fair-haired youth may a pitfall be.*
> *He, too, must cross in the twilight dim;*
> *Good friend, I am building this bridge for him."*

The challenge is this: Don't just become a fellow Rugged; become a Rugged Bridge Builder who is committed to encouraging and empowering other potential Ruggeds.

Rugged False and Fast Starts

Here's a look at how some very successful Rugged companies and Rugged Entrepreneurs performed in their first year of business. Some as you will see, started big and got bigger; others prevailed despite initial failure, and still others hit the ground running and never stopped. I hope you find inspiration in them all!

- In his first year in the automobile business, Henry Ford went bankrupt. Two years later, his second company also failed. His third corporation, however, has done rather well.
- Bank of America was destroyed in its first year of business by the 1906 San Francisco earthquake. But founder Amadeo Giannini rescued $80,000, set up a plank bank on the waterfront, and loaned out money to help rebuild the city, requiring only a man's pledge as security.
- Dr. Seuss's first children's book was rejected by 23 publishers. The 24th publisher sold six million copies of it.
- In its first year in the soda business, The Coca Cola Company sold only 400 Cokes.
- The Apple microcomputer was turned down by both Hewlett-Packard and Atari before achieving first-year sales of $2.5 million.

- In 1903, King Gillette invented the safety razor but sold only 51 razors and 168 blades. Today it is the bestselling safety razor on the market.
- In 1765, repairman James Watt designed the world's first steam engine in only two days, but it took him ten more years before he could produce the first working model.
- During his first year at Harvard, Edwin Land dropped out of school and went home, where he then invented the Polaroid.
- Howard Hughes Sr. was forced to abandon his first oil well because he couldn't drill through the hard rock. He then founded Hughes Tool Co. and invented a rock drill that became the foundation for the family fortune.
- In its first 28 attempts to send rockets into space, NASA had 20 failures.
- In their first attempt at finding oil, Edward Doheny and Charlie Canfield dug a shaft 165 feet into the La Brea Tar Pits in Los Angeles and struck just enough oil—seven barrels a day—to finance their Union Oil Co.
- In his first year out of college, Isaac Newton completed his major life's work in gravity, the nature of light, and calculus.
- In his first year on the professional golf circuit, Jack Nicklaus won the U.S. Open.
- In their first year as recording artists, the Beatles had four songs that made it to #1 on the charts.
- In 1891, American Express invented the traveler's check and sold $9,200 worth of them. It became a product that generated billions of dollars and allowed American Express to borrow funds at a negative rate of interest. Today, traveler's checks are almost nonexistent, but American Express's Platinum card is among the best among travelers for the bonus mileage it encourages.